Caring for Your Family Treasures

Heritage Preservation

Caring for Your Family Treasures

Heritage Preservation

Text by **Jane S. Long** and **Richard W. Long**

General Editor, **Inge-Lise Eckmann**

Project Director, **Clare Bouton Hansen**

Foreword by **Lawrence L. Reger**

Abrams, New York

Editor: Harriet Whelchel
Designer: Carol Robson

Library of Congress Cataloging-in-Publication-Data

Long, Richard W.
    Caring for your family treasures : heritage preservation / text by Richard W.
Long and Jane S. Long ; general editor, Inge-Lise Eckmann ; project director,
Clare Bouton Hansen ; preface by Lawrence L. Reger.
    p. cm.
    Includes index.
    ISBN 13: 978-0-8109-2909-8 (pbk.)
    ISBN 10: 0-8109-2909-0 (pbk.) / ISBN 0-8109-4147-3 (book club: hc) / ISBN 0-8109-2987-2 (book club: pbk)
        1. Antiques—Conservations and restoration. 2. Collectibles—
        Conservation and restoration. I. Long, Jane S. II. Eckmann, Inge-Lise.
        III. Hansen, Clare Bouton. IV. Title
NK1127.5.L66 2000
745.1'028'8—dc21
                                    00-29300

Printed and bound in China
10 9 8 7 6 5 4 3 2

Pages 2–3: Country Kitchen;
and pages 22–23: reading room,
designed by Meg and Steven
Roberts, The Echo Design
Group, Inc.

HNA
harry n. abrams, inc.
a subsidiary of La Martinière Groupe

115 West 18th Street
New York, NY 10011
www.hnabooks.com

Contents

Foreword

In the 1960s, my mother embarked upon a crusade to create photograph albums and scrapbooks in an attempt to document and preserve our family's memories. Using the magnetic albums available to her at the time, she thought she had found a way to keep these irreplaceable items safe and available for telling stories to future generations. Little did she know that, thirty years later, the albums would have discolored and irreparably harmed many of those images.

Lawrence Reger with his parents, 1943

As we work today to preserve treasured family objects—whether they be Grandfather's rocking chair, Mother's wedding dress, or Uncle Bob's stamp collection—we have unprecedented access to information and products unavailable thirty years ago. In fact, there are so many products for any need and answers to nearly any question as to be overwhelming. The challenge is finding the right information and the safest materials.

And so this book.

For years, professional conservators have guided museums and libraries in caring for precious collections held in the public trust. Their knowledge and methods are based on scientific research into how objects deteriorate over time. Professional conservators are experts, "doctors" for collections, who not only bring about "cures" but also, and more important, advise on how to give our family treasures "total fitness" and long life.

When we published *Caring for Your Collections* in 1992, our goal was to give private collectors, small museums, and historical societies access to expert advice. At the time, some pamphlets and articles on specific objects were available, but no single comprehensive volume existed. For its era, *Caring for Your Collections* was a breakthrough.

Caring for Your Family Treasures represents the next step. It is at the same time both simpler in content and broader in scope. It brings to your home the best preservation advice professional conservators have to offer. Thanks to our Project Director Clare Bouton Hansen, you will also find many delightful photographs assembled from our Heritage Preservation family and a useful appendix to guide you.

Crossing into the new millennium has caused much ado about determining what is valuable from our past and what to take with us into the future. We know we cannot keep everything, and deciding what to keep is not easy. In the end, the things we choose to hold onto become that much more precious to us, and it is important that we care for them properly.

Caring for Your Family Treasures will be an indispensable tool in making sure your treasures are on hand for future generations.

Lawrence L. Reger
President, Heritage Preservation

Caring for Your Family Treasures

Family Treasures:
Links to the Past

Most of us are so busy living our lives that we cannot imagine making time to gather a family history. On a special occasion we may take a photograph, recount a story, or ask a relative to tell us a special memory. Some of us are by nature collectors and act as family historians by keeping treasured objects. We can make these objects more meaningful by documenting our stories and deciding which are truly significant. These recollections, dreams, and discussions we share with loved ones are themselves gifts.

Precious objects carry the experience of meaning, and this meaning grows with time. I recently moved across the country. When I unpacked the soup tureen my grandmother brought to the United States seventy years earlier, I felt new respect for her courage, and I could better understand her experience of immigrating. I remembered the story of my grandparents watching all their belongings being lifted off the ship in New York harbor, one crate falling onto the dock and shattering the coffee and dessert china. Within a few years my grandmother would be a widow and head of a young family. The wedding porcelain that survived would carry memories of holidays, birthdays, and special dinners for our entire family.

Family celebrations are a wonderful opportunity to record memories. Consider keeping an album illustrated not only with photographs but also recipes, music, and handwritten cards and letters. Videotaping is also an excellent way to document history, but it is important to keep the process simple and not intrusive. Encourage the retelling of stories, which are both familiar and new each time they are retold.

Documenting our lives seems a little like packing away holiday ornaments at the end of the season. Putting things in order may not seem exciting, but if you look at the process as wrapping gifts for the future it can be very satisfying.

Perhaps the most difficult part of building a history is the selection process. Acting as curators for our history, we have to be discriminating. Knowing what is most important today is difficult, but understanding what was meaningful to our forbears and what might be significant to future generations is an even greater challenge. Keep in mind that if we try to save too much, it will be impossible to care for it all. One approach is to ask yourself what one object you might save if you had to evacuate your home. People often feel that family photographs are most valuable, but each of us has our favorites, and discovering what these are can be a great treasure hunt.

Once you have selected your treasures, you have to determine how to keep their meaning alive. It may not be prudent to continue regular use, but it may be worth the risk involved to display and use an object for special celebrations. Evaluate the risks in handling or displaying of an irreplaceable object. Try to evaluate how fragile, repairable, and valuable your object is. You may wish to study the conservation and collection literature noted in the appendix of this book, or consult a conservator or appraiser. Professional recommendations are helpful but, in the end, only you can evaluate the risk of losing something of personal significance.

In the following section, "An Ounce of Prevention," you will find information on a few key preservation principles, such as careful handling, controlled light exposure, and stable temperature and relative humidity. Stability is especially important when you consider that artifacts from the deserts of ancient Egypt and the bogs of northern Europe came down through the centuries preserved in extreme opposite but constant environments.

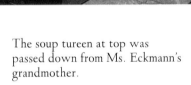

The soup tureen at top was passed down from Ms. Eckmann's grandmother.

Seventy years later, the tureen graces the dining table and keeps family memories alive.

Page 10:
We can't stop time and the natural deterioration of objects, but we can slow the pace of deterioration through proper care and protective measures.

As a conservator myself, I would like to add a personal word about an important principle: first, do no harm. Most frequently, damage occurs during handling. Always plan ahead, use clean hands, and have a safe place prepared to set down whatever you are handling. Severe damage can also happen when you are attempting to clean or repair. Helpful friends and advice columns will offer a host of home remedies. Beware! Damage from inappropriate restoration is often irreversible, and many people have come to me in distress after unwittingly damaging their precious objects. For example, one common folklore remedy recommends the cleaning of paintings with a potato or onion. These raw vegetables might remove some surface grime, but not without risking abrasion and leaving damaging residue. Caroline Keck, noted conservator and educator, quipped that one might well use this technique to clean little boys—but for the violent protest. Intervention by an inexperienced hand usually complicates problems. Often the best preservation effort you can make is to keep objects you value in a stable environment and handle them with care.

The ambition of *Caring for Your Family Treasures* is to help you develop a thoughtful, commonsense approach to reducing the risks to your cherished possessions. The advice in this book is based on the knowledge and experience of experts from respected institutions such as the American Institute for Conservation of Historic and Artistic Works; Canadian Conservation Institute; Colonial Williamsburg Foundation; Conservation Center for Art and Historic Artifacts; Historic New Orleans Collection; Library of Congress; Minnesota Historical Society; Museum of Fine Arts, Boston; Museums and Galleries Commission (U.K.); National Park Service; Nebraska State Historical Society—Gerald R. Ford Conservation Center; Northeast Document Conservation Center; Smithsonian Institution and the University of Delaware/Winterthur Museum Art Conservation Program.

In our culture there is a myth that the new is inherently better than what came before. As we reflect on the richness of the past and the century just beginning, we can shape our legacy by preserving our treasures for our families.

Inge-Lise Eckmann
Chairman, Heritage Preservation

An Ounce of Prevention Is Worth a Pound of Cure

Just as early screening and detection are effective means of preventing major medical problems, preventive care of your treasures will save you the cost of conservation treatment or, worse, losing an object. A basic understanding of the forces of deterioration and principles of safekeeping will arm you with the knowledge of how an ounce of preventive maintenance and ongoing care is worth a pound of cure.

Agents of Deterioration

Almost everything changes with time, either subtly or dramatically. Both overt and invisible forces are constantly causing deterioration. An object's composition, its environment, and its use all contribute to how it withstands the test of time. A summary of the agents of change and how they affect objects follows.

Composition

Some materials simply last longer than others. Ceramics and stone are inherently more stable, while textiles and paper are more susceptible to deterioration. Organic materials that come from plant or animal sources are more fragile than inorganic materials. For this reason alone, great-grandmother's vase is likely to be in better condition than her handbag.

"Brittle paper," a phenomenon attributed to acidic wood-pulp paper, literally breaks apart.

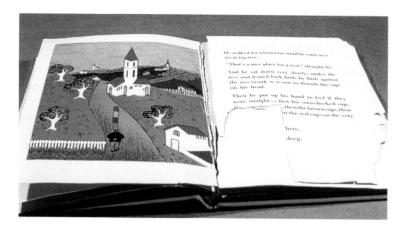

Other materials are prone to damage from a characteristic flaw called *inherent vice*. For example, many common wood-pulp papers produce acid as they degrade, creating "brittle paper" that crumbles to the touch. Early photographic film made from nitrocellulose forms acids as it ages and deteriorates.

Construction techniques can also affect an object's susceptibility to damage. Methods of furniture construction can restrain wood in a way that causes splitting or permanent constriction of wood fibers as the wood shrinks and swells. Sometimes the combination of different materials leads to damage, as metal of one kind in contact with another can cause electrolytic corrosion, or the chemicals in leather can corrode metal.

ORGANIC/INORGANIC

The materials that make up your family treasures can be classified as either *organic* or *inorganic*. Organic materials come from living things. These plant and animal sources contain cellulose and protein. In general, organic materials are more fragile and vulnerable to damage from humidity, light, and pests than inorganic materials are. Inorganic materials such as metals, stone, ceramics, and glass are generally more durable, but they are not immune from deterioration.

Environment

Fluctuations in relative humidity, extreme temperatures, pollutants, and exposure to light can all damage objects.

Extended periods of high relative humidity (over 65 percent) and elevated temperatures court danger by promoting mold and mildew and accelerating chemical deterioration. Mold and mildew can attack any organic matter and flourish in high relative humidity. Not only do these fungi stain objects, they can also destroy the organic fiber itself.

Temperature and Relative Humidity

Warmth and moisture also promote chemical reactions that cause metals to corrode, plastics to soften, and photographic emulsions to become sticky. As the temperature and relative humidity rise, more moisture becomes available for these reactions. In fact, the rate of a chemical reaction doubles for every rise in temperature of 18 degrees Fahrenheit.

Alternately, at relative humidity below 30 percent, organic materials can begin to desiccate, causing fibers to shrink and distort. Just as the use of heat in winter causes your skin to feel dry, it can affect objects adversely. Paper, textiles, and leather may become dry and brittle. Wooden objects and furniture may crack and split. Glues may weaken, causing joints to open and veneers to peel.

Mold can attack any organic material and will flourish in high relative humidity.

Rapid or frequent fluctuations in relative humidity create stress as materials change shape. Alternately absorbing and losing moisture increases internal stresses in materials such as wood, paper, and fabrics. At some point, fibers lose their malleability and splits or cracks develop. Composite objects are perhaps most dramatically affected because different materials absorb and lose moisture at different rates, resulting in buckling, splitting, or flaking.

Strive to maintain a moderate, stable relative humidity. Museums monitor temperature and humidity with sophisticated instruments called hygrothermographs. Simpler equipment is adequate for home use, and a wide variety of instruments for any budget can be purchased through conservation and other suppliers. These range from inexpensive humidity-indicator cards that change color, to expensive digital units that provide instantaneous and precise readings. The museum ideal of 72 degrees Fahrenheit, 50 percent relative humidity may not be practical in the home, particularly in climates that are predominately arid or humid. The key is to avoid extreme fluctuations and provide a relative humidity that is as constant as possible. Human comfort is a good indicator in general, and the living areas of your home are probably already fairly constant. Hence, it is easy to understand the admonition of not storing precious objects in the attic or basement. You are probably also unconsciously aware of the relative humidity swings caused by open windows and doors as well as dampness brought in from the rain and snow. Mud rooms and vestibules are designed to buffer extreme swings in temperature and humidity, thereby lessening the swings

in interior spaces. Hence, they are not good locations for cherished
photographs, fine paintings, or heirloom furniture.

Pollutants are everywhere: soot in the smoke from your fireplace,
pollen blowing in through the window screen, fumes from the
cleaning solution you use on your kitchen floor, acids emitted by unsealed wooden shelves. Solid particles can mar
surfaces through abrasion. Gaseous pollutants create corrosive chemical reac   **Dust and**
tions such as the tarnish on silver. Acids, **Pollutants**
ozone, and sulfur dioxide can build up and
break down fibers in textiles, papers, and photographs.
These harmful effects are magnified in closed spaces such as
drawers and cabinets where the pollutants become more concentrated. Ordinary plastic bags and cardboard boxes can emit
acids and additives that will deteriorate and stain objects they
hold. For these reasons, good housekeeping practices and the use
of chemically stable storage materials, such as inert plastic bags
and buffered and unbuffered boxes, are critical to the good health of
your heirlooms.

Tarnish on silver is perhaps the
most familiar example of the
effects of gaseous pollutants on
family treasures. Storing this cof-
feepot with a sulfur scavenger
will minimize tarnish.

Signs of animal and insect pests include droppings (called frass),
sawdust, casings, holes, and nesting materials. Warm, damp conditions together with dirt will encourage infestations.
The best protection is good housekeeping. Check your   **Pests**
living and storage areas regularly. Close gaps that allow four-legged
friends access. Eliminate sources of water and food. Be careful when
first bringing objects into your home since you may not readily
detect the presence of eggs, larvae, or bugs. Museums carefully

examine and sometimes isolate new objects to be sure they are bug free before putting them on display or in storage where they can contaminate other objects.

Any signs of insects or pests should be investigated immediately. If you see a moth, find the source immediately before generations feast on your treasures. Many infestations and outbreaks have grown into a major problem because they were left undetected in dark storage areas. Early detection through regular inspections can prevent or mitigate such damage. When a pest is detected, approach eradication judiciously. Use the most gentle means of control possible. Responding with pesticides and other chemicals may cause irreparable harm to your treasures. If an infestation is detected, consult with a conservator for the best means of eradication.

The pervasive use of sunblock has made us all aware of the damaging potential of light. Three types of light can damage objects. Visible light can fade dyes and furniture finishes. Ultraviolet radiation (UV) is the most energetic form and can break down the fiber structure of organic materials. Infrared radiation produces heat that can accelerate fading and chemical deterioration.

Light

Some materials and dyes are more light sensitive than others. The effects of light are cumulative; thus, limiting light exposure overall can prolong an object's original appearance. One effective way to reduce light exposure is simply to close the blinds. Another way is to turn lights off when you are not around. UV light is not necessary for human sight and can be filtered from sunlight and fluorescent bulbs. Incandescent and halogen bulbs produce damaging heat, so use the lowest wattages possible near treasures. Many museums now use fiber-optic lighting because it has no UV light and does not generate heat. But this may not yet be practical for home use. Keep in mind that short-term exposure to high levels of light with ultraviolet radiation can cause as much damage as long-term exposure at a lower level of light. "Resting" an object by removing it from light exposure will not reverse damage already done, but it will prevent new damage.

BUYER BEWARE

As you shop for materials to help you care for your treasures, you will discover that many products are labeled as "acid-free," "preservation safe," or "museum quality." Be aware that these terms are not standardized and may be misleading. Even the term "archival quality" can be misused. Products that are acid-free today may develop damaging acids as they age. It is most important to be sure that materials you use are chemically stable. Specially prepared paper products that are labeled "unbuffered" are suitable for most materials, and products labeled "buffered" are appropriate for particular types of artifacts. (For guidance, refer to Finding Materials and Tools on page 141.)

The fading effects of light are dramatically apparent when the mat board is removed from this watercolor.

Use

Use of any object will cause wear and tear over time. Sometimes the signs of wear add to the object's history and beauty, like a fine patina. Most often, however, wear and tear reduce the value of an heirloom or even destroy its beauty and function. Enjoy your treasures, but use them judiciously if you hope to pass them along to future generations. Consider how you use your treasures. Are they used annually on special holidays? Or once in a generation in a cere-

An example of one collector's treasures, thoughtfully displayed and well maintained.

mony? Perhaps they are sat upon every day. Frequency of use should be factored into decisions about storage and display methods.

Use necessitates cleaning, and inappropriate methods or materials can damage your treasures. Detergents and soaps can leave harmful residues. Scrubbing can abrade and scar objects. Even dusting with a cloth can scratch and mar surfaces. Beware of the desire to return objects to a like-new appearance. Rather, learn to appreciate the signs of use and wear as part of the object's unique history and sentimental value.

Repeated or careless handling of an heirloom increases the risk it will be damaged. In turn, improper repairs can cause more harm than good.

Who isn't tempted to mend a small tear with that handy roll of tape in the kitchen drawer? Resist this urge because self-adhesive tape leaves a sticky residue that can stain and disfigure any surface it contacts—including paper, furniture finishes, fabrics, even ceramic glazes. Home remedies for removing white rings on furniture can ruin the finish. Even repairs made by some self-proclaimed experts can cause damage. Improper materials used to fill holes in wooden furniture can create stresses that cause the surrounding wood to crack.

On the other hand, when a cherished object is not in use or on display, don't neglect it. Inspect stored objects regularly for signs of mold, mildew, rodents, and insects.

Principles of Safekeeping

Here are some principles to guide you in keeping your treasures safe:

If you are comfortable, your objects will be comfortable. When you feel hot or cold, damp or dry, so do your treasures. You wouldn't be comfortable living in the basement or attic; neither are they. You feel better when there is good air circulation; so do they.

Avoid extremes of temperature and relative humidity. Strive to maintain as moderate and stable a level (72 degrees Fahrenheit and 50 percent relative humidity) as practically possible. When choosing where to display or store objects, remember that the conditions of interior walls, rooms, and closets are more stable than those on the exterior.

Create micro-climates and use protective covers. Matting and framing with proper materials create a protective micro-climate, as do chemically stable boxes (even boxes within boxes). Use dust covers on stored objects and polyester liners on wooden shelves to protect your treasures from dust and pollutants.

Limit light exposure. The damaging effects of light are cumulative. Take precautions with the amount and type of light to which your treasures are exposed.

Inspect your treasures regularly. Regularly checking your treasures will help you monitor and tend to problems as they arise. A water condensation problem might not be present in the summer but, left unattended during the winter, could cause serious damage. Likewise, early detection and elimination of pests is less costly and harmful than a full-blown fumigation.

Respond promptly. The speed with which you respond to a problem can diminish the severity of the resulting problem. Immediately blotting a fresh spill on a cotton tablecloth, then flushing with water is better than allowing a stain to set, thereby necessitating the use of harsh soap or detergent later.

Use the gentlest means possible. Blot, don't rub. Brush, don't scrub.

Avoid do-it-yourself repairs and treatments. When in doubt, consult a professional conservator.

Be sure that any alterations are reversible. Respect the original historic materials and structure. Don't cut an artwork to fit a frame. And if you must clip a photograph for your scrapbook, do it to a copy and keep the original intact elsewhere.

This teapot was damaged and repaired in the early twentieth century using metal straps. With modern adhesives, repairs are no longer so obtrusive. Modern conservation practice is guided by the principle of reversibility so that treatments may be undone as better methods and materials develop.

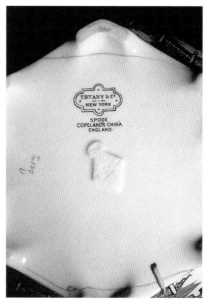

Guardians of Family Memory

Guardians of

Family Memory

Books

Does it afflict you to find your books wearing out? I mean literally. . . . The mortality of all inanimate things is terrible to me, but that of books, most of all.

—William Dean Howells, letter to Charles Eliot Norton

Books play many parts in our lives. They entertain and inform. Some, like the family Bible, record the story of our family. Beautifully bound books are works of art and, as is the case with unblemished first editions, can be valuable. Depending on the quality of the original paper and binding, well cared-for books can grace a room with their beauty and increase in value for many years.

Even the most elegant books are mostly paper. Some paper is short lived but other kinds have surprising endurance. Since 1860, when publishers began using paper made from wood pulp rather than rags, the physical quality of books has varied widely. Paper high in wood-pulp content is very acidic. It will discolor, dry out, and begin to crumble into dust within years, or even months in the case of newspapers. Books made of poor-quality paper have a limited future, no matter how new or how well bound and cared for. With proper attention, a book printed on good paper—ideally acid free—has the potential for a long life.

Keeping Your Books Healthy

Proper care of books means protecting them from several hazards. The greatest threats are mold; the deterioration of paper hastened by exposure to certain chemicals or environmental conditions and animal or insect pests; and damage to the structure or binding of the book.

Passing down favorite books is a marvelous way to link generations.

High relative humidity and warm temperatures encourage the growth of mold. Once mold develops, it is extremely hard to control. The same conditions, as well as frequent rapid fluctuations in temperature and relative humidity, stimulate chemical reactions that increase the rate of deterioration of paper. The primary cause of damage is acidity. The best protection against mold and acid damage is to keep your books at a constant, moderate temperature and relative humidity. Extremely low relative humidity also can cause problems, particularly brittleness. The temperature should be no higher than 75 degrees Fahrenheit and the relative humidity should be as close to 50 percent as possible.

Excessive light is another hazard for books. Prolonged, direct exposure to bright light from any source, but especially direct sunlight, causes fading and accelerates the chemical reactions that make pages, bindings, and even dust jackets deteriorate. You shouldn't store books in basements, attics, or unheated buildings, nor should you keep them close to heat vents, radiators, hot lights, or fireplaces.

Make sure air can circulate around books, and remove grit, pollen, and urban dust frequently. Valued books should be dusted carefully, opened, and inspected for mold or signs of pest infestation at least once a year. You can vacuum them on low suction, with the brush attachment covered by cheesecloth secured with a rubber band.

Two examples of good storage for books. *Left:* This box has been fitted with foam to house a small book. The box can stand on end and be shelved with larger volumes.

Right: A custom-fitted phase box will protect this book for years to come.

Proper handling and display are important for preserving the life of a book. Here are some pointers on how to keep your books healthy while you continue to enjoy them. Book lovers always remove a book from its shelf by pushing back the books on either side, then grasping the spine between the thumb and fingers and pulling the book out. Many books have been damaged by pulling them by one finger at the top of the spine.

The structure of an old book may be weak. Don't force it open too far, and turn the pages with care. Leaving objects in books—things like rubber bands, flowers, paper clips, self-adhesive notes, newspaper clippings, and even book marks—risks harm. These everyday objects can cause discoloration, rips, and even chemical damage.

Except for oversize volumes such as atlases, family Bibles, and coffee-table books, it's best to keep your books standing upright, with another book of similar size or a bookend on each side. Books should not be packed too tightly together on the shelf, and there should be a few inches of open space behind them to allow air to circulate. Exposure to fresh air retards deterioration, so occasional careful handling is actually good for a book.

The wrong way to remove a book from the shelf. Pulling at the top of the spine will cause damage. The correct way is by holding the front and back cover between thumb and fingers in the center of the spine.

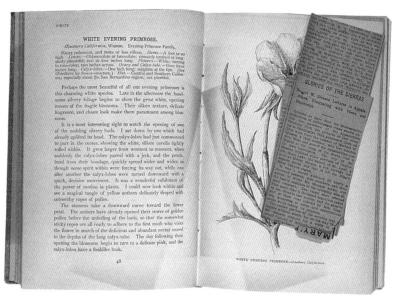

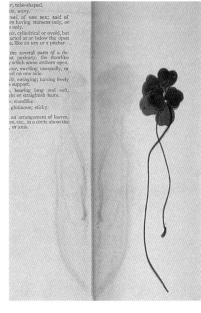

Anything left in a book—whether to mark a place, preserve a keepsake, or retain additional information—can leave a trail. *Clockwise from left:* The paper clip has caused staining. Acid from this newspaper clipping has migrated to the pages in the book and resulted in discoloration. Pressed flowers and leaves can have the same effect.

Because wood, even treated wood, contains natural acids that react with paper and accelerate its deterioration, glass shelves or metal shelves that are powder-coated or coated with baked enamel are preferable to wood. But if you enjoy the warmth of wooden furniture, a reasonable compromise is lining shelves with polyester film or heavy, acid-free paperboard.

A book on display—not shelved with other books—needs special care. Most important, never force a book open too wide; be sensitive to signs of resistance. If it is displayed open, the book should have support beneath both sides so that the spine is not under stress. If the top is raised to make the book more readable, there should be

Improper support has allowed these book pages, also known as the *text block*, to pull away from the cover. Be sure to provide adequate support when handling and displaying books. Similarly, never force a book open.

support along the bottom edge so that the weight of the book is not pulling against its cover. Change the open pages frequently so that one page is not exposed to light for long periods. A case made with ultraviolet-filtering acrylic glazing instead of plain glass will help protect a book on display. But the case should allow air circulation and should not collect heat or moisture. Bright spotlights should not be used because of the potential for damage from heat as well as light.

Repair of Damaged Books—A Job for a Pro

The repair of damaged books and bindings is a special skill in which professional book conservators are trained. The wisest course for book repair is to consult a professional conservator before taking any measures that might ruin a book. Damaged books should be stored in acid-free boxes or wrapped in acid-free paper held together with cotton twill tape. Cellophane or other pressure-sensitive tape should never be used on paper or bindings. The adhesives deteriorate faster than the book and will discolor and otherwise harm the paper. Once used, adhesive tapes are very difficult to remove without risking further harm.

LEATHER BINDINGS

Until recently, leather book bindings were customarily treated with oil to reduce drying. Long-term studies now suggest that applying oil or other treatments probably does more harm than good to books and their bindings. It may cause the binding to become sticky or gummy. Rough calfskin and suede will darken if oil is applied, often spotting or staining unevenly.

It is inadvisable to oil vellum or parchment; these materials will discolor if they are exposed to any form of moisture. There is also a risk that oil will seep through the cover and damage the pages.

The effects of treatments vary, depending on the material used to make the binding and how it was cured, so it is best not to use any oil, polish, dressing, or saddle soap unless you are advised to do so by a conservator who has examined your book.

The use of a rubber band to hold these deteriorated books together has further damaged both the pages and cover. Instead, place a damaged book in an acid-free box or wrap it in acid-free tissue tied with fabric tape.

Recovery from water damage requires patience and a gentle touch. Drying treasured objects too quickly can lead to new disasters.

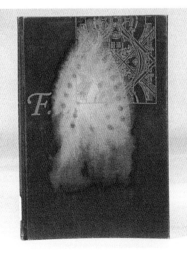

These clothbound books with machine-stamped decoration date to the 1830s. They are valued in the marketplace as interesting objects rather than for their contents.

Caring for Books: A Checklist

✓ Keep books at a constant, moderate temperature and relative humidity

✓ Dust and inspect books for pests at least annually

✓ Protect books from exposure to bright light, especially the sun

✓ Hold books with fingers along the spine

✓ Keep the pages of your books free of foreign objects

✓ Shelve books upright with books of similar size on both sides

✓ Store large or heavy books lying flat

✓ Protect books from direct contact with wooden shelves

✓ Never use tape to repair books or covers

✓ Never oil, "dress," or polish bindings

Family Treasures on Paper

Sir, more than kisses, letters mingle souls;
For, thus friends absent speak.

—John Donne, verse letter to Sir Harry Wotton

The highlights of personal and family history are usually recorded on paper. Births, graduations, marriages, military service, occupational licenses, and deaths are memorialized on paper certificates. Other paper records and mementoes enrich family history by information they provide or events they symbolize. Old letters, journals, invitations, maps, ticket stubs, cards, stock certificates, expired passports, graduation programs, report cards, and newspaper clippings are interesting, often fun to read. Troves of old family papers sometimes contain treasures such as a letter from a famous person or an ancestor's recollection of an event of historical significance. Whether they are important for history, valuable to collectors, or a pleasure for the family, it makes sense to keep family papers in the best possible condition.

The principal elements of family papers are, simply, paper and ink. Both range widely in durability. Paper was first made by the Chinese from pulped scraps of cloth thousands of years ago. The technique has

Frakturs are pieces of decorative calligraphy done in a Pennsylvania Dutch style. This *fraktur* not only documents a family event, it is a work of art.

evolved a bit but, as in ancient times, fine paper made by hand of cloth pulp without chemical additives has a potentially unlimited life expectancy—if it is well cared for.

Few people today routinely use top quality, handmade paper for family documents. Most of the paper we consider good is less stable than we assume. Chlorine is employed to bleach the inexpensive rags used to make even relatively high-quality modern papers, but chlorine causes chemical reactions that make the paper less durable. Since the middle of the nineteenth century, more and more paper has been manufactured using wood pulp, which is less expensive than used rags. This type of paper is sized with chemical compounds that, when exposed to heat and humidity, generate sulfuric acid. Very acidic paper, that used in most newspapers and "pulp" novels for example, will become brittle and yellow in a matter of months; in the sun, the timeframe is reduced to a matter of days! Even the best care will not preserve for long family documents printed or written by hand on such paper, but at least you can save the contents by making a photocopy.

The durability of ink also varies depending on its composition. Iron gall ink, used in pens in the eighteenth and nineteenth centuries, can fade when exposed to light; the sulfuric acid it contains attacks and embrittles paper. Some inks cause writing to "migrate" through the page or onto adjoining pages over time, producing the appearance of smudges or shadows. Contemporary writing inks—especially those used in markers and felt-tip pens—are even more unstable. Documents written in pigment ink rather than dyes are much less likely to fade.

Collecting family papers can be a pleasure, sometimes important for the sake of history. If your collection is large, you may enjoy organizing and cataloguing it. The principal threats to family papers are similar to the hazards faced by books. They are: exposure to certain chemical and environmental conditions, careless handling, mold, and animal and insect pests such as mice, silverfish, and cockroaches.

Extremes in temperature or relative humidity—and frequent fluctuations in either—are harmful to paper documents. High relative humidity and temperatures encourage the growth of mold, and, like frequent changes in temperature and relative humidity, stir the chemical pot, hastening deterioration. Very low relative humidity

Personal letters provide a wonderful glimpse of days past. They can bring an unmet ancestor to life as a photograph cannot. Note the ink migration, a natural chemical process.

causes paper to become brittle. Light, especially direct sunlight, also energizes the harmful chemical processes.

Excessive and improper handling is another threat to family papers. Letters and documents that have been repeatedly folded and refolded deteriorate rapidly and break on the fold lines. Oil left on paper from handling by many human hands discolors documents, and frequently used documents often get smudged with dirt or grit. Papers stored without periodic care, including inspections, may become an expensive delicacy for a variety of insects and rodents.

Keeping Family Papers in Top Condition

The best protection you can provide against mold and brittleness is to keep your papers at as constant a moderate temperature and relative humidity as possible for you. Papers will thrive in about the same conditions as books: a temperature no higher than 72 degrees Fahrenheit, with relative humidity close to 50 percent. Obviously, it is not a good idea to store important papers in a damp basement or an attic or garage that is too hot in summer and too cold in winter. Keeping papers in climate-controlled parts of the house has the added advantage of reducing the risk of insect or animal damage.

It is best to keep loose papers laid flat and unfolded in acid-free paper or polyester folders, and to keep the folders themselves in acid-free boxes. That is because the acid in wooden boxes or very

A comparison of proper (*above*) and improper (*top*) ways to hold paper. Provide support so there is no stress to the paper that might cause damage.

acidic paper can spread into your documents if they come in contact. For that reason, it also is best to store newspaper clippings away from other documents. Best of all is to photocopy newspaper articles or any material that is on poor quality, pulp paper onto acid-free paper.

Large documents such as diplomas or maps need support, which can be provided by oversized, acid-free mat board. The entire document should be completely covered, top to bottom, to protect all parts from steady exposure to light, sticky fingers, spills, and the like. Rubber bands, staples, paper clips, glue, and cellophane adhesive tape all damage paper over time; you should avoid using any of these things, but glue and tape are especially harmful. See the chapter on

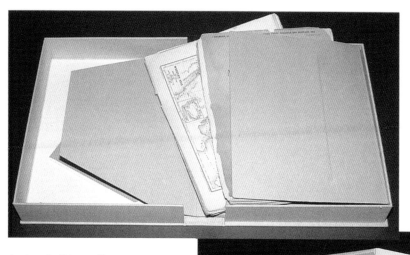

A clamshell box allows delicate papers to be stored flat while providing support and protection. This box comes with an attached stiff sleeve that holds the papers in place.

Acid-free, archival enclosures will help preserve family papers for the future.

matting and framing (page 61) for suggestions on safe adhesives.

Taking care of family papers is relatively simple. It is best to keep them in the condition you find them, using the guidelines discussed. Harder may be avoiding the temptation to make permanent fixes or minor repairs that most often prove harmful in the long run. Lamination seems like the answer to a prayer when it comes to preserving documents. Unfortunately, it is quite harmful to paper over the long run and irreversible. It is better to encapsulate a document in a stable plastic storage sleeve, available from conservation suppliers. Deacidification is very risky, a process best left to professionals.

Repairing tears with transparent tape or glue is also extremely unwise. The adhesives quickly discolor paper and are difficult if not impossible to remove without causing further damage. Starch paste applied sparingly can be used for repairs (see the formula for starch paste on page 64). Dirty or moldy paper can be treated, but that, too, is a job for a professional.

Caring for Your Family Papers. A Checklist

- ✓ Keep papers at a constant, moderate temperature and relative humidity
- ✓ Store papers in darkness; expose them to light— especially sunlight—as little as possible
- ✓ Fold and unfold letters and other documents as little as possible
- ✓ Store loose papers unfolded in acid-free paper or polyester folders
- ✓ Separate highly acidic paper like newspaper clippings from other materials
- ✓ Photocopy contents from highly acidic documents onto acid-free paper
- ✓ Don't laminate important papers
- ✓ Leave deacidification to professionals
- ✓ Don't use paper clips, rubber bands, tape, or glue on important papers

These maps show the damage of folds and adhesive tape. They are now properly stored flat in polypropylene envelopes.

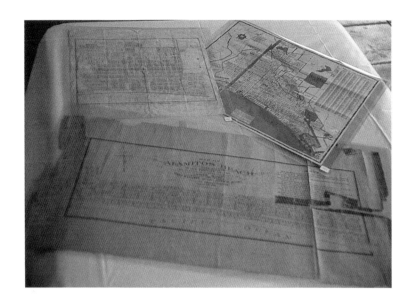

A Note about Art on Paper

Every home has works of art on paper. Your family may not have a drawing by an Old Master or a Picasso lithograph but you probably have a child's picture, framed magazine illustration, map, or a sketch in pencil, crayon, or charcoal. In fact, far more paintings and drawings are done on paper than on canvas: for example, pastels, watercolors, or pen and ink drawings.

Depending on how the paper was made and how it is cared for, a work of art on paper may have a long and happy life or a short, inglorious one. A major factor in the durability of art on paper is the structure and properties of the paper, a subject discussed in more detail earlier in this chapter. Another is the care it is given. Destruction of the paper itself is the major threat to art on paper. The most common villains are acidity, exposure to excessive light, and mold or mildew.

Unless you are prepared to pay for expensive treatment, there is little that can be done if acidity resulting from the manufacturing process is causing the paper to discolor and deteriorate. However, the acid damage caused by contact with cardboard or other mounting materials with high pulp content can be avoided. Light in the ultraviolet range is so destructive to drawings and paintings on paper that conservators recommend no pictures be left on display permanently. Museums, for example, try to rotate items on display every three months. Light not only hastens deterioration of paper, it also causes fading, particularly in watercolors and pastels. If you want to display your watercolor, it is best to protect it with ultraviolet filtering glass or acrylic. Consider hanging it where you need to turn on a light in order to see it. Ordinary incandescent lights do not emit harmful rays, but since they get hot, they should be kept at a safe distance from the art.

High temperature and high relative humidity accelerate deterioration of paper and encourage the growth of mold and mildew. Fluctuations in temperature and relative humidity are also undesirable because they may cause cockling or undulations in the paper. Many old prints are marred by foxing, brownish stains in the form of spots. Foxing can result from fungi, the chemical components of the paper, or moisture. You cannot reverse the process, but you can stop the stains from getting worse. Keep the temperature in a room where paper works are stored or displayed below 72 degrees Fahrenheit and the relative humidity around 50 percent. Use a room dehumidifier if necessary.

There are other hazards to works of art on paper. Some paintings or drawings, particularly pastels and charcoal drawings, smudge easily on contact. The bright, glossy paper of contemporary prints and posters is vulnerable to staining by the touch of oily, or even slightly dirty, fingers. Don't touch works with bare hands; use clean cotton gloves.

It is wise to frame valued works of art on paper so they can be displayed without the risk of damage from direct handling. Framing is a critical step. Done properly, matting and framing protect the art and increase its life. But if the job is done incorrectly or if the wrong materials are used, irreparable harm can be done. Please refer to the chapter on matting and framing for more detail (see page 61). More damage is inflicted on pictures, especially works on paper,

This nineteenth-century print exhibits a variety of problems. It is discolored from exposure to light. It also shows evidence of foxing, which most likely resulted from elevated relative humidity. Finally, it has been stained by an acidic mat. Note how a cover paper the mat was wrapped with protected the print where it extended just a few millimeters under the bevel.

by incorrect mounting and framing than by any other cause that is under our control. Be sure to avoid using pressure sensitive or self-adhesive tapes.

If your works of art are not framed, they should be stored individually between layers of protective matting or in folders. Whichever holder is used should be made of lignin-free, buffered stock and be firm enough and large enough to provide support for the entire work. Edges of works that stick out will soon fade or be torn or stained. Make sure that the protected storage piece is laid flat. The perfect storage place is a specially designed case called a Solander box. Acid-free boxes or anodized aluminum or powder-coated steel drawer units also work well, but it is best not to use an untreated wooden cabinet or drawer because wood can transmit acidity and resins to paper.

A Solander box is an ideal way to provide support and protection to a delicate work of art on paper while it is stored flat. It is slightly sturdier than most clamshell boxes.

Scrapbooks
and Albums

I have more memories than if I were a thousand years old.

—Charles Baudelaire, *Les Fleurs du Mal*

Scrapbooks often hold the most personal clues to a family's history. Bits of paper, ribbon, and news clippings mark the milestones of generations—births, graduations, weddings. Postcards and theater programs celebrate trips and special events, and elaborate valentines and pressed flowers evoke romances from an earlier day. Old scrapbooks and albums are more important than the sum of their contents. The way they are assembled and the choice of material for inclusion make them unique family documents.

Because scrapbooks and their contents—greeting cards, stamps, ticket stubs, and snapshots—represent a variety of components, materials, and shapes, they pose a challenge for preservation. The covers may have raised surfaces and be composed of leather, cloth, plastic, or paper. The various contents can be made of textiles, paper, hair, or flowers. Greeting cards and small souvenirs might feature three-dimensional decorations or even moving parts. These mementos are sometimes unique, often fragile, and always of sentimental value.

This photograph of the author and his mother is imperiled by the "magnetic" album in which it is displayed. Note the discoloration of the album page.

Hazards

The most common ingredients of scrapbooks and albums are photographs and other kinds of paper materials bound in various ways, sometimes just as books. You might want to refer to the other chapters on books, family papers, and photographs for a better understanding of how each of these materials should be cared for. In general, the same hazards threaten them all: extremes in temperature and relative humidity, acidity, prolonged exposure to light, mold, pests, and careless handling.

There are, however, a couple of problems peculiar to scrapbooks and albums. Sometimes the albums themselves are a menace. In many old photograph or stamp albums, for example, the pages are made of highly acidic black construction paper or dark card stock. Postage stamps and photographs also may have been fixed with glues that are liable to stain the images. Likewise, the newer "magnetic" albums—the type with sticky pages covered with plastic—are very harmful to photographs and should not be used. After a few years, the contact adhesive becomes visible along the edge of the pages, and the discoloration eventually spreads under the plastic to the photographs. Removing photographs may require professional help because they may tear.

Contents can be a problem as well. Newspaper clippings and other papers that are highly acidic can be a further threat to mementos.

Many old albums have black pages, which are highly acidic. Note how these album pages are very brittle because they were made from wood-pulp paper. The dyeing process used to color the paper may also contribute to its embrittlement. The postcard, on the other hand, is in good condition because it was made from rag pulp.

Pressed flowers not only soil papers but are also a temptation to insects. Preserve them separately in rigid acid-free folders. Paper clips and staples are also hazards since they can cause rips and rust stains.

Prolonging the Life of Family Albums

Keep scrapbooks, as well as photograph and stamp albums, in the same stable environment as you keep your favorite books. Avoid exposure to extremes in temperature and relative humidity, sunlight, and dirt. Inspect them regularly for signs of mold or pests.

There are also some specific steps you can take to prolong the life of your family album and the memories it holds. Detaching photographs from acidic album pages can be risky. If papers or photographs are firmly attached to the pages, place sheets of acid-free

Though this album is on highly acidic black pages, the precious line drawings warrant keeping it intact. Interleaving the pages with acid-free, buffered paper will help prevent acid migration. However, be aware that the increased bulk will create stress on the spine. Good care means balancing risks and protecting the historic integrity of family treasures.

paper or polyester film between pages to help protect the mementos. This is called *interleaving*. Just be aware that the extra bulk created by the addition of these sheets will put stress on the binding. Do not force the covers closed.

If a scrapbook already contains acidic materials like news clippings, remove them, *if you can do so safely*, and then carefully make two photocopies of each on acid-free paper. Take special care in handling the acidic paper, which may be brittle. Put one acid-free copy into the album, place the other in your files, and save the original in an acid-free sleeve. Papers with signatures, annotations, or other handwritten information may be an exception. In those cases, consult a conservator about keeping the originals in the scrapbook. If you cannot remove the acidic items safely, use the acid-free sheets described above to separate the "hot" items and improve the overall environment in the album.

Staples and paper clips can be detached from album pages or documents safely by sliding a thin, stiff piece of plastic under the fastener on both sides of the document. Slide the paper clip off the plastic; for staples, use a pair of tweezers or thin knife to straighten the staple ends and pry out the staple. The plastic will protect the paper from abrasion and from damage by your tools. A regular staple remover can tear papers.

Enjoying Your Scrapbooks and Albums

Always handle an old scrapbook or album with care. Support the binding and pages while you hold it, and be careful not to fold or crush items when you are turning pages or closing the book. Mementos or photographs should not protrude from the edges of the book after it is closed. Shelve small and medium-sized scrapbooks and albums upright. Albums that are large, bulging open, or filled with loose items should be kept flat or displayed in a book cradle. Never place bulging scrapbooks on top of each other, and never stack more than three closed albums.

Most scrapbooks and ephemera can be stored according to the general guidelines for family papers. Scrapbooks that are of special historic or sentimental value should be stored individually in custom-fitted boxes. Unbound ephemera should be sorted by size and type—photographs or letters, for example—and then individually enclosed to protect them from acidity or careless handling.

Creating family scrapbooks has become a very popular pastime, and many stores now specialize in materials to enhance the presentation of family photographs and souvenirs. When you make history, make it last: choose preservation-quality materials, such as acid-free paper for pages and stable plastics for sleeves, pocket pages, and stamp mounts.

A modern album made of proper materials is an excellent way to store historic memorabilia as well as photographs.

Top right: An album stores postcards in polyester sleeves, allowing a view of both the image and message.

Above: Here a handsome collection of hand-made Christmas cards through the years.

Right: This acid-free, archival-quality album preserves both the content and original script of a treasured family recipe.

TIPS ON MAKING A NEW SCRAPBOOK OR ALBUM

1. Use only stable plastic or acid-free paper corners to attach items.

2. Handle photographs and papers only by the edges and as little as possible. Wearing clean cotton gloves will protect your treasures from dirt and oils.

3. Be sure that photographs are labeled on the back or on album pages. Use a soft (no. 2) pencil or photo-marking pen and write lightly.

4. Photocopy newspaper clippings or other acidic items onto acid-free paper and put the copies into the album.

5. Original photographs, postcards, military ribbons, or other memorabilia can lose their value when cut into decorative shapes. Use copies to make decorative displays.

6. Take care not to mangle photographs or historic documents in scanners or copy machines.

7. If you are making a stamp album, keep the postage stamps in polyester sleeves. Retaining and protecting the adhesive on the stamps will add to their worth.

The photographs in this old album were processed into decorative shapes. If you wish to clip images into decorative shapes when making a new photograph album, do so to a copy print. Keep the original, whether historic or modern, intact in a separate location.

GENEALOGY AND FAMILY TREASURES

A family's genealogy and its treasures are interwoven. More than one genealogist has come across old newspaper accounts of the wedding of beloved grandparents with a description or photograph of the bride's dress while tracing family history, and later found the very same dress carefully stored away. Family Bibles and family papers—military-discharge papers, baptismal certificates, deeds, land claims, report cards, and the like—often contain important clues for genealogical research. Knowledge of genealogy, on the other hand, may explain and substantially increase the interest of some heirlooms that have passed down through the family. A sideboard made in New England in the eighteenth century now resides in the family place in Missouri. It has even more meaning as a family heirloom if we know that certain ancestors brought it with them when they migrated by covered wagon from Virginia in the early nineteenth century.

Just as every person has a genealogy, whether or not it has been researched and recorded, so all objects have a *provenance* (a history of where they originated and where they have been), whether or not it has been documented. In fact, the value of an antique or art object is substantially affected by how well its provenance is documented. Objects that can be traced back to their origin, whether from the studio of an artist or from a factory, are more certainly genuine than objects whose history can't be traced. Consequently, they are of much greater financial value. Provenance has also become increasingly important with regard to the legal status of certain archaeological and ethnographic objects.

Genealogical research and record keeping relates family history to objects and documents. Linking this grocery ledger to the grocer in the photograph makes both keepsakes more meaningful.

A historic album can be beautiful as an artifact in its own right. This photograph album from c. 1870 has a leather cover with a metal closure; the leaves are gilded along the edges. This particular album is optimally stored in an acid-free box.

Some conservation suppliers offer storage boxes and acid-free sleeves made specifically for mementos such as postcards and stereo views. Others can produce custom-sized enclosures in quantity to meet special needs.

It may be tempting to repair an old scrapbook yourself, but amateur repairs can do more harm than good. If individual items are loose but the album is sturdy, reattach photographs and mementos using only plastic or acid-free paper corners. Never use tapes, glues, or other commercial adhesives. If the photographs or souvenirs are of special value, just keep the album and its contents safe until you can consult a conservator about repairs. A scrapbook cover that is separating can be tied loosely with linen or cotton fabric tape to keep it secure; center the knot on the front cover. If the book is damaged, wrap it in acid-free paper or keep it in an acid-free box.

Caring for Your Scrapbooks and Albums: A Checklist

✓ Get professional help to remove photographs from self-adhesive albums

✓ In albums with acidic pages or self-adhesives, interleave photographs and other precious items with acid-free sheets

✓ If acidic materials like news clippings can be safely removed, carefully photocopy them onto acid-free paper. Put copies into the scrapbook and your files

✓ Always handle old scrapbooks and albums gently

✓ Shelve small and medium-sized scrapbooks and albums upright; store them flat if they contain loose items or are large or bulging open

✓ If the cover is loose, tie the book with linen or cotton fabric tape; store damaged albums in acid-free boxes

✓ Never repair scrapbooks and albums with tape. Use only plastic or acid-free paper corners to reattach loose items

✓ Store postage stamps in polyester sleeves

Photographic Prints
and Transparencies

To collect photographs is to collect the world.

—Susan Sontag, *On Photography*

The oldest pictures in many family albums are studio photographs of great grandparents, formally posed, often with the wife standing with her arm draped across the shoulder of her seated husband. Such portraits are evidence of the growing prosperity and technological development of late nineteenth-century society. Along with the candid images of family gatherings, automobiles, vacation trips, and the like that fill our albums and shoe boxes, these old photographs mark some of the profound social changes that have taken

Photographs of our ancestors are often formal studio portraits.

These wedding photographs (c. 1890 and 1920) illustrate how the increasing portability of cameras affected the style of imagery over time.

place in the twentieth century. Our increasing mobility is reflected in the subjects of pictures as well as the evolution of our cameras—from studio models, the Brownie, the Polaroid, and the single-use camera to the digital camera. Family history is American history. Collections of prints and slides, and family albums with pictures accumulated over most of the century, are a major source of historical and biographical information as well as family fun.

While the equipment has evolved and the fashions of the subjects have changed, the motives for taking and saving photographs remain the same. Taking pictures, sharing copies with friends, and arranging photographs for display are in themselves enjoyable activities for many people. More fundamentally, we share our ancestors' desire to capture in an instant the significant events, places, and people in our lives. Many people regard family photographs as among their most prized possessions. But photographs—even those taken within the last ten years—can fade away without proper care.

The underlying structure of photographic prints is similar to that of paintings. The image itself is usually silver, platinum, or organic dyes or pigments. It rests in a transparent binder layer—usually made of albumen, collodion, or gelatin—which is attached to a primary support, most commonly paper. Each component layer is subject to natural deterioration and particular hazards.

This hand-colored nineteenth-century albumen print is especially vulnerable to fading.

Several hazards threaten photographic prints, negatives, and color transparencies (often in the form of 35 mm slides). High temperature and high relative humidity hasten the natural processes of deterioration and provide a good environment for mold or mildew, which can damage your prints by attacking the binder layer. Bright light, especially ultraviolet light from the sun or other sources, causes fading and hastens chemical reactions that accelerate deterioration. Rodents and certain insects are fond of some of the ingredients commonly used in the binder layer. Given the opportunity, they will make a meal of your prints.

Photographic prints may also be harmed by exposure to certain chemicals found in mounting materials, albums, or the boxes or envelopes in which they are stored. Exposure to acidified paper or glue of any sort is especially harmful. Dirt and the oil found naturally on human skin also damage photographic prints, slides, and negatives.

These photographs exhibit severe damage from the glue used to hold them in an album.

Keeping Photographs Bright and Clear

Since it is normally the content of the picture rather than one specific print or slide that is significant, it is important to take very good care of negatives and to make duplicates of pictures you value. This is particularly urgent for damaged or deteriorating photographs and those you want to display. Though there is usually at least a slight loss of quality in a copy, the clock on the process of natural deterioration starts over. Having a good copy also allows you to store the original under conditions as nearly ideal as possible. Ideal conditions include a cool, dry, and light-free environment. For a black-and-white print, a temperature of 68 degrees Fahrenheit and relative humidity of 30 percent to 40 percent are ideal. Negatives, contemporary color photographs, and slides benefit from a cooler environment when that is possible, but with the same low relative humidity.

Pictures should be enclosed in an envelope, album, or folder to protect them from dirt and bright light. Acid-free paper or chemically stable, polyester film such as Mylar D® is best for storing prints. Because they may give off gases that are harmful to prints, negatives should be stored apart from photographic prints or slides, in buffered archival enclosures. Color transparencies are best kept in stable polyester sleeves. Be sure that photographs are not stored in contact with brown wrapping paper, glassine envelopes, mounting board containing acidic wood pulp, rubber cement, or glue. All of those things contain chemicals that are harmful to photographic prints.

Albums made with acid-free paper are a good way to store and display photographs. They create the opportunity to label photographs clearly and provide a useful context for pictures. A photograph album can be fun as well as an invaluable source of historical information, but avoid self-adhesive (sometimes called "magnetic") albums since they are prone to discolor and cause damage to prints (see the chapter on albums and scrapbooks, page 38, for more detailed information).

If you choose to store photographs in acid-free envelopes or folders, these should be kept loosely filed, not packed tightly, in acid-free boxes. Each photograph should be labeled lightly but clearly on the back in soft (no. 2) pencil indicating when it was taken, where, and names of the people in the photograph. Using the full name is preferable to nicknames or relationship terms such as "Gramps," as such references quickly become obscure. Rather than labeling in detail on the back, you can number prints or slides and keep a corresponding record with descriptions in each storage box. Keeping the same descriptive information for negatives is especially important.

The more you handle photographs, the greater the likelihood they will be damaged by oily fingerprints or dirt. When it is necessary to touch them, photographs and negatives should be handled by the edges, and slides should be handled by their mounts. It is a good idea to wear clean white cotton gloves when setting out on a sorting or mounting project that will involve handling many photographs.

When displaying a photograph that will be constantly exposed to light, protect the print behind ultraviolet filtering glazing such as UF-3 Plexiglas®. Color photographs are particularly subject to fading, so it is not a good idea to display them for long. All photographs should be mounted on acid-free matboard that passes the Photographic Activity Test (PAT). PAT is actually a series of tests that measure the reaction of photographic images to materials with which they come in contact (refer to the Glossary, page 147, for further information on PAT).

Examples of museum-quality housing for photographs and daguerreotypes. Some of these enclosures have been custom fitted.

If a photograph is to be framed by a professional, it is a good idea to take a list of specifications for materials with you to the framer and to make sure that the framer is willing and able to do the work with the proper materials. See the chapter on matting and framing for a description of the appropriate supplies.

The temptation to make home repairs to a torn or cracked photograph is sometimes compelling. It is better to place such a picture carefully in a polyester sleeve supported by acid-free matboard. If the picture is flaking or has been treated on the surface with a brittle or crumbly coloring or tint, do not use a sleeve. Rather, place it

CARE OF DAGUERREOTYPES, TINTYPES, OR AMBROTYPES

Nineteenth-century photographs with the image on a metal or glass primary-support base—daguerreotypes, tintypes, or ambrotypes—have characteristic susceptibilities of their own and should be treated with extreme care. Daguerreotypes consist of a silver-plated copper base with a silver/mercury/gold amalgam image. They were often hand colored with pigments. The highly polished silver surface of daguerreotypes is easily damaged by airborne moisture and pollutants; however, the surface should never be cleaned or even touched because such treatment will inflict permanent damage. If you are considering restoration work on these kinds of photographs, you should consult a professional conservator.

Many daguerreotypes and ambrotypes are still in cases supplied by the photographer. If the case is intact, it should be stored flat in a drawer. If hinges are broken, the case should be bound together with cotton or linen tape. If the photograph is not in a case, it should be stored lying flat in a closed clamshell box. Nothing should touch the surface. Tintypes, which are often found loose, should be housed in acid-free or polyester folders and boxed away from moisture.

Because daguerreotypes are produced on silver or silver-plated copperplates, they can become tarnished. This daguerreotype was so badly tarnished the image was not visible. A professional conservation laboratory removed the photograph from its case and electrolytically removed the tarnish, then replaced the cover glass and resealed it in the original case.

in a shallow box by itself. Do not use transparent self-adhesive tape for any repairs. The tape will discolor quickly—it actually deteriorates more rapidly than a photographic print—and the adhesive will cause irreversible damage.

You can clean a soiled photograph carefully with a clean dry soft brush from the center outward toward the edges. Do not use water or solvent-based products such as window cleaners. Improper cleaning can cause permanent staining or loss of the image. Lamination also is irreversible and will ultimately destroy a photograph. Consult a professional conservator before undertaking any procedure with the potential to change a photograph you wish to keep.

Caring for Your Photographs: A Checklist

✓ Store photographs and slides in a cool, dry place with a minimum of light

✓ Use acid-free—not magnetic or self-adhesive— albums

✓ Display copies of photographs while keeping originals safely stored

✓ Protect slides in stable polyester sleeves

✓ Store photographs and negatives in envelopes or folders made of polyester or acid-free paper and file them loosely in acid-free boxes

✓ Avoid storing photographs or negatives in contact with brown wrapping paper, glassine envelopes, mounting board with high wood-pulp content, rubber cement, adhesive tape, or glue

✓ Be alert to clues of the presence of rodent or insect pests

✓ Avoid touching photographs, negatives, and slides; handle them by the edges

✓ Wear clean cotton gloves when you work with prints, negatives, or slides

✓ Display photographic prints behind ultraviolet filtering glazing such as UF-3 Plexiglas®; use acid-free mats that pass the Photographic Activity Test (PAT)

Three good ways to store slides: in carousels, in polyethylene sleeves, and in slide drawers.

Home Movies:
Videotape and Film

*Some memories are realities, and are better than anything
that can ever happen to one again.*

—Willa Cather, *My Antonia*

Videotaping has become very popular with the advent of portable cameras. Use tapes that are short in length to make your prized videos. Shorter tape has a thicker base and is more resistant to wear.

Americans have always loved the movies. Years ago, many children spent Saturday afternoons at the matinee and today videocassette players are an integral part of home entertainment systems. Some families have impressive collections of films dating to the 1920s. Moving pictures have also been a popular way to chronicle family history. Whether we used the movie cameras of the 1950s or the ubiquitous camcorders of the 1990s, we all shared the desire to capture baby's first steps or the flight of the bridal bouquet.

Unfortunately, magnetic tape—including both videotape and audiocassette tape—is not the most permanent medium for preserving a family's history for the long run. It is more fragile than black-and-white photographs. Even when it is stored under ideal conditions, videotape may last only a few decades. Some optical disc technologies, such as CDs, promise a lifetime of one hundred years, but that may mean little, as recording and playback systems are likely to become obsolete much sooner.

Hazards

Videotape has three basic components: magnetic particles, a polyurethane binder, and a polyester base material for support. All these elements are subject to irreversible damage when exposed to extremes of temperature and relative humidity, pollution, careless handling, or poor storage conditions. Storage at high temperatures can result in image dropouts, which appear as flashes or streaks. Exposure to direct sunlight can cause the reels or cassette housings to warp. High relative humidity may facilitate mold growth; dust and pollution can result in a loss of both video and audio signals.

Prolonging the Life of Your Tapes

There are ways to help make videotapes—and family memories—last. The most important step is to copy your most valued video- and audiotapes and, when appropriate, transfer them to new technologies, for example having an eight-track stereo recording copied onto a compact disc. Take tapes in poor condition or obsolete formats to experts equipped to duplicate or reformat them. Make at least two copies of videotapes: a preservation master copy and a copy for viewing. The preservation master should be of the same or higher quality than your original, most likely a professional format like Betacam SP or Digital Betacam. The lowest quality format is VHS, but it is fine

Machine-readable media present preservation challenges as they are replaced by newer technologies. Access to the information they contain becomes more difficult as their playback equipment becomes increasingly hard to find and service.

for regular use. It is a good idea to have your videotapes professionally copied every ten to fifteen years. The preservation master or extra copies of the most treasured tapes should be stored at a separate location, such as in a safety deposit box or the home of a relative.

Good basic care can help to preserve precious images and sounds. The environment for video- and audiotapes should be dust free, with the temperature about 68 degrees Fahrenheit and the relative humidity around 40 percent. Cleanliness is important, so regularly clean your VCR or other playback device and follow recommended maintenance procedures. Protect VCRs with a dustcover. Videotapes, especially modern ones, are fairly impervious to the weak magnetic fields produced around television sets and other electrical appliances; however, it is best to keep prized tapes at least a few feet away from electrical machinery and not to stack them on playback equipment.

Handle cassettes as little as possible and do not touch the surface of the tape. Insert and eject tapes at blank, unrecorded sections, and pause the tapes as little as possible. Remove tapes from players or rewinders right after use, and rewind them soon after playing. Avoid playing valuable tapes on unfamiliar or suspicious playback devices.

Store reels and cassettes standing on end, like books, in protective, plastic containers. Keep them in cool, dry, dust-free areas away from direct sunlight. Play and rewind valuable tapes that are in storage at least once every three years. Playing relieves stress on the tape and gives an early warning of any problems.

TIPS ON MAKING NEW MEMORIES

When you videotape a special event, use a new tape from a highly rated manufacturer. The shortest running tape should be used for important recordings because the base will be thicker and more durable. When possible, choose the SP (standard) speed over the EP (extended) mode. Break off the tab on the videocassette to prevent accidental over-recording. After making a recording, rewind the tape before ejecting it. If the event is truly important, take a few black-and-white photographs as well.

LPs, CDs, AND RELATED MEDIA

You may have a classic record collection or may be compiling a family history on a compact disc. In general, avoid touching the playing surfaces and keep the recordings in a stable environment away from bright light. If you are uncertain about playing back a recording, consult a professional. Below are a few additional suggestions for extending the life of these treasures.

Cylinders. Pick up cylinders by inserting your middle and index fingers into the center hole. Avoid touching the grooves. Wax cylinders should be at room temperature before you handle them. Store them on edge.

Grooved Discs (78s, 45s, LPs, and Acetates). Touch grooved discs only on their edges or on the label area. Shelve them vertically on a support strong enough to handle their weight. Most record jackets should be replaced with sleeves of high-density polyethylene, a kind of plastic that is frosted and will feel slick. The original sleeve may have liner notes or other valuable information. You can store both the record in its new sleeve and the old sleeve inside the original jacket. LPs can be cleaned with a water-based record-cleaning fluid, but 78 rpm records should only be dusted, as water or alcohol-based cleaning fluids may damage them.

Compact Discs. Handle compact discs only by the outer edge or center hole. Shelve them vertically. To clean CDs, use a very soft cloth and the moisture from your breath and wipe in a radial motion from the center to the edge.

Handle reels of film as little as possible. Grip them only by the frames at the center and the edges.

Most original record sleeves should be replaced with polyethylene sleeves to preserve the recordings.

Motion-Picture Film: Old Films and Home Movies

Some families have collections of older films produced for showing in theaters. While some of these are dangerously flammable (see warning opposite), later commercial films and virtually all home movies are on "safety" film stock. With time, motion-picture film will fade and deteriorate to varying degrees and at varying paces.

Cellulose nitrate film was first made in 1889 and used primarily between 1900 and 1939. Its production was gradually phased out, although some was available as late as 1951. Movies on nitrate film should be copied and replaced immediately for reasons of safety as well as preservation. Consult with a conservator for the names of commercial labs equipped to make good duplicates.

The unevenness that has developed from playing and rewinding this reel-to-reel tape will distort the sound and eventually damage the tape structure.

Like nitrate film, acetate film (also known as safety film) can decompose rapidly if it is stored under poor conditions, although it is not truly flammable. A strong vinegar smell is a sign that acetate film is decomposing. Most 8mm and 16mm color home movies are made on Kodachrome® film stock, produced by Kodak after 1940. Kodachrome® film stock has tended to fade less than the tricolor-pack film prints used commercially since the early 1950s.

The sooner copies are made of old films, the more likely their contents will be preserved. An older film may have torn sprocket holes or may have shrunk, making it difficult to play back. A copy can be made onto videotape for viewing, but the original film should be kept, if at all possible, for making future copies. Even damaged, the film is likely to outlast a current videotape.

Careful handling and storage can extend the life of any type of safety film. Handle older films as little as possible and then only by the edges. Always rewind

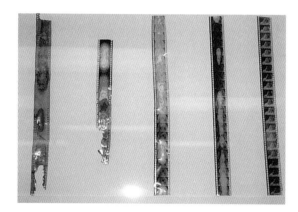

Some examples of nitrate negative film self destructing. Nitrate film can decompose rapidly and is highly flammable.

WARNING:
Nitrate film is highly flammable and cannot be extinguished once it starts to burn. If you think you may have nitrate film, seek advice from a specialist. If you are certain you have nitrate film, contact your local fire department for advice on immediate disposal.

DIGITAL INFORMATION: IMAGES, SOUNDS, TEXT, MULTIMEDIA, AND WEB PAGES

Images, sounds, texts, or other multimedia presentations are recorded digitally on electromagnetic media such as computer diskettes or hard drives or compact discs. They can be reproduced with superb quality if good equipment is used at both ends of the process. Pictures made with a digital camera and sound files on recordable compact discs have the added advantage of allowing instant review, on the spot retakes if necessary, and electronic portability across the Internet. Theoretically, the codes from which a digital file is built do not degrade when they are copied.

But there are downsides to digitization. Not all scanners or digital cameras produce high-quality images; on the contrary, most current home-generated digital images are poor. The media on which the digital codes are embedded are impermanent and have the same problems as other magnetic media such as videotape. Of more concern, the technologies and formats for reproducing pictures and sounds digitally are evolving rapidly. Eventually a de facto standard does come to dominate

The process of digitization results in a loss of detail that is highly variable, depending upon the dots per inch (dpi) within the scanned image. Compare these images scanned at 150 dpi (*left*) and 600 dpi (*right*). In the preservation field, digitization is considered a means by which to access information. It is not a substitute for original materials.

each field, at least for a time. But newer technologies overtake those standards fairly quickly. If you use current technology and want to keep today's digital images accessible for the future, not only will you have to protect the discs or diskettes on which digital files are stored, but also, as technologies change, you will have to make sure that your electronic files migrate into contemporary media and formats. You will need to remain alert and act promptly to make sure your images or sounds are not stranded in obsolete technology.

Many libraries, museums, and archives are in the process of digitizing major parts of their holdings in order to increase access to their fragile collections. This is not intended to replace the original materials. Access is an important consideration for families as well.

You may want to scan your photographs into electronic files to send to friends via the Internet, or copy important letters or other documents as backup. If so, be careful of small, auto-feed scanners that can chew up photographs and documents. If a photograph or document is precious to you, carefully scan it only on a flat-bed scanner, where the risk of harm is minimal. If you are interested in making an electronic record of a document or photograph for more than casual purposes, you will need to use a top-quality scanning device, which will build a very large electronic file. The file can be stored on an optical disc such as a recordable CD. Mediocre scanners or scanners set to minimize file sizes will make poor images, lacking in resolution and even detail.

Web sites, home pages, and e-mail also pose interesting questions for those who would like to preserve family history. Their most obvious purposes are transitory: to communicate basic information for a relatively short period. But they are also a social and, in a few cases, an artistic phenomenon. Considerable creativity has been invested in many home pages, and e-mail has supplanted note and letter writing for some people. The kind of information many family home pages contains is likely to be of interest to family members in the not too distant future, and certainly to social historians long term. But Web pages and e-mail are extraordinarily ephemeral. Future historians are not likely to have more than a few random samples of these communications from our time. Keeping an electronic copy of the various parts of a Web page is a complex undertaking. A Web page on a particular day includes many files, some in different formats. Many of these files are constantly changing.

If it hasn't happened already, it probably won't be long before someone proudly shows you an electronic copy of Sally's first Web page—preserved for posterity. In a time of experimentation and rapid change, the best ways to do that are not yet clear, but there is little doubt that ingenuity will prevail.

film evenly and not tightly, with the emulsion side out. At minimum, film should be stored at temperatures around 68 degrees Fahrenheit and less than 50 percent relative humidity. Ideal storage temperature and relative humidity are even lower, depending on the type of film. Store films in metal film cans or plastic boxes of uniform size and shape. The films should be stored lying flat, in stacks never more than one foot tall. Paper or foreign objects should never be left in storage cans with film; film cans should be labeled on the outside with information on the contents—the date, film size, subject or title of all segments, and length. Decomposing acetate films with a vinegar odor should be stored away from each other and other films.

Caring for your Videotapes: A Checklist

- ✓ Take valuable tapes in poor condition or obsolete formats to experts equipped to reformat or copy them
- ✓ Make at least two extra copies of your precious tapes—a master and a viewing copy—and store the master at a separate location
- ✓ Keep tapes in cool, dry, dust-free areas, away from direct sunlight and a few feet from sources of magnetic fields
- ✓ Clean and perform specified maintenance on playback devices at the designated intervals; use dustcovers to protect them
- ✓ Never touch tapes, especially the surfaces
- ✓ Insert and eject tapes at blank points; pause tapes as little as possible
- ✓ Rewind tapes soon after playing; remove them from players or rewinders right after use
- ✓ Avoid playing valuable tapes on unfamiliar or suspicious playback devices
- ✓ Store reels and cassettes standing on end, like books, in protective plastic containers
- ✓ Use good quality (shorter, thicker, and stronger) tapes for important recordings
- ✓ Break off the tab on a videocassette to prevent accidental over-recording

Matting and Framing
Your Treasures

A little amateur painting in watercolor shows the
innocent and quiet mind.

—Robert Louis Stevenson, *Virginibus Puerisque*

Framing can really bring out the beauty of a piece and, when done correctly, can protect it for years to come.

You can extend the life of your family treasures by carefully selecting the materials you use to mount or frame them. This is true for works of art and other family treasures on paper, as well as photographs, textiles, and cultural artifacts. First, you might want to examine prized art that is already matted or framed. Acidic matboard, brown backing paper, and cardboard will hasten the decay of prints, photographs, and paper objects.

If any work that you value is matted with such harmful materials, you should have it rematted immediately, along with newly discovered treasures you want to mount and display. Always put an identifying mark on the item you are mounting or framing. Any paper-based treasure can be labeled along the edge on the back with a no. 2 pencil. If a letter or other historically important document associated with an artwork exists, it should be properly preserved as a treasure in its own right.

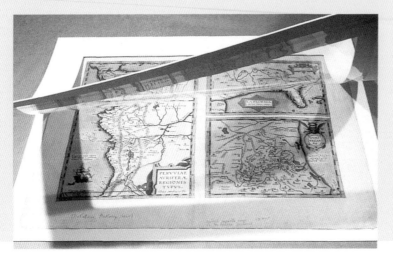

Whether you decide to do the framing yourself or use a professional, always choose the safest materials. If you take your treasures to a framer, choose a reputable business and specify the kinds of materials you want used. Both the mat—the "window" surrounding the front of the picture—and the backing board that supports it, should be acid-free and lignin-free.

Don't dry-mount paper because paper moves naturally as its moisture content changes with variations in relative humidity. Instead, you can mount paper using a high-quality Japanese paper hinge affixed along the top edge with a non-staining adhesive. You can order wheat-starch paste from a conservation supplier, or make a safe homemade paste as described in the formula given on page 64. Use paste sparingly. Acid-free paper or polyester photo corners can be used to mount smaller objects. Commercial adhesives are very harmful to paper. Never use spray mount, rubber cement, pressure-sensitive backing, or adhesive tapes. They will eventually cause irreversible discoloring and will deteriorate faster than your object.

If you have your art framed and glazed, make sure the window matting is thick enough to prevent the glazing from coming in contact with the picture. Glazing should be done only with glass or acrylic sheets (e.g., Plexiglas®, Acrylite®, Lucite®, Perspex®, and Lexan®). However, acrylic sheets develop static and should not be used if the art is flaking or is of a powdery medium such as chalk, pastels, or charcoal. Both glass and acrylic can be purchased with added ultraviolet (UV) filtering to reduce the damaging effects of

Above left: This map is properly supported by a larger piece of matboard. The hinged window mat allows viewing while providing protection.

Above right: This watercolor, its mount, and mat were stored loose in a drawer where they were not held together well. The acidic mat shifted and you can clearly see how it damaged the paper. Regrettably, the damage closely encroaches the actual image.

This drawing was attached to its backboard with glue. Because the adhered portion cannot change in response to fluctuating humidity, as the unadhered portion can, severe undulations have resulted. Restricting the movement of paper with tape causes the same problem. Works of art should be hinged to the backboard.

The tape applied to the back of this document left a disfiguring mark. To make matters worse, the owner tried to remove the tape residue with lighter fluid, which resulted in the "tidemark" stains.

sunlight and fluorescent and halogen lamps. However, acrylic UV-filtering material is more effective than the glass.

Frames can be either wood or metal. Frames should have enough strength and depth to hold the work. An extra layer of museum board, held in place on the back of the framed work with stainless-steel or brass brads, will protect the art from airborne pollutants and dirt. When handling a work of art on paper for framing, as at other times, it is best not to touch the work directly but to wear clean cotton gloves.

This detail shows insidious water damage to a frame that was stored in a damp basement.

QUICK WHEAT-STARCH PASTE

A starch-based paste can be made at home from either rice starch or wheat starch (*not* flour, but the starch extracted from the wheat or rice flour), which can be purchased through conservation-supply catalogues. This paste, prepared in the microwave, is used by many paper conservators when they need to work with only small quantities.

Place 1 tablespoon wheat or rice starch in a
    microwave-safe container.
Add 5 tablespoons of distilled water.
Microwave on high setting 20 to 30 seconds.
Remove container from microwave and stir the
    paste.
Microwave another 20 to 30 seconds; remove
    container and stir again.
Continue this process several times until the
    paste is stiff and translucent.
Cool paste before using.
Note: If larger quantities are made in the
    microwave oven, increase the cooking time
    between stirring.

The consistency of the paste you need will depend on the particular task. A texture similar to toothpaste is adequate for most mending. Practice with the paste before using it on your work. Brush it back and forth on blotter paper using a no. 4–bristle brush to make a thin layer of fairly dry paste. The paste can be diluted with distilled water to achieve the consistency required.

Starch paste should not be refrigerated; cover and store it in a cool, dry place. It will keep only for a week or less. If the paste discolors, develops dark flecks or a sour odor, which indicates mold, discard it immediately.

Two types of hinges for mats. If the edges of the item will be covered by the mat, the work can be attached with (a) hangers of hinging tissue adhered to the mat with white gummed cloth and to the artwork with wheat-starch paste. If the edges are to be shown, a (b) folding hinge can be used.

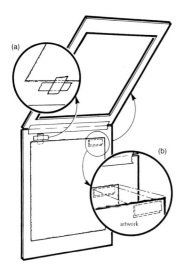

Matting and Framing: A Checklist

✓ Put an identifying mark on an item you are having framed; a paper-based treasure can be labeled along the edge on the back with a no. 2 pencil

✓ Use a window mat or spacer to keep the object from touching the acrylic or glass

✓ Use only acid-free matting and backing boards; acidic matboard, brown backing paper, and cardboard will hasten the decay of prints and photographs

✓ If the original is stiff enough and not too large, use acid-free or polyester photo corners to attach it to the backing; if you cannot use photo corners, apply Japanese paper hinges with wheat-starch paste

✓ Never use spray mount, rubber cement, pressure-sensitive backing, or self-adhesive tapes

✓ Protect the image with acrylic glass or sheets that filter ultraviolet light; use only glass for artworks in powdery mediums like chalk, charcoal, or pastels

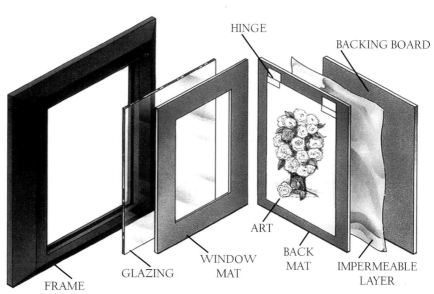

The elements of a properly matted and framed piece

HINGE

BACKING BOARD

ART

BACK MAT

IMPERMEABLE LAYER

WINDOW MAT

GLAZING

FRAME

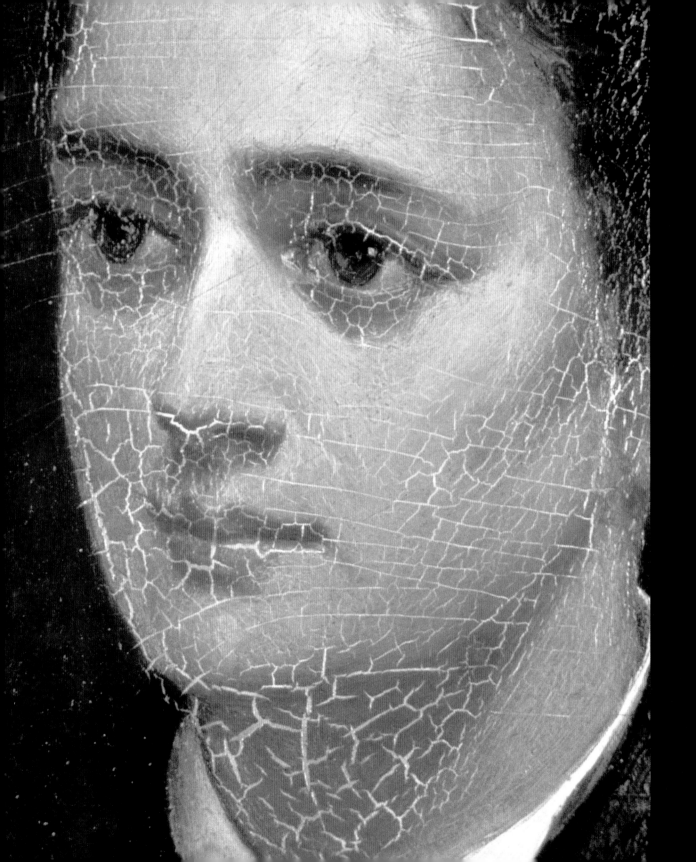

Tangible Legacies
Tangible Legacies

Paintings

We're made so that we love
First when we see them painted, things we have passed
Perhaps a hundred times nor cared to see;
And so they are better, painted—better to us,
Which is the same thing. Art was given for that.

—Robert Browning, *Fra Lippo Lippi*

Painting is a romantic art. The reading public knows a good deal about the lives of many great painters—from masters like Michelangelo to modern bohemians like Henri Toulouse-Lautrec. Art thefts, lost paintings, forgeries, and restorations are avidly covered by newspapers and have been the subjects of popular books and movies. Family portraits and other heirloom paintings are treasures far beyond monetary measure for families lucky enough to possess them. Some families own museum-quality oil paintings, and many more have excellent pictures by nineteenth- and

early twentieth-century or contemporary artists, many of whose works command steadily increasing prices. Paintings by family members or friends hang in many American homes as well. An original painting impresses its special character, as well as the taste of its owner, on the room in which it hangs.

A great deal of time and effort have been invested in studying the chemistry and structure of oil paintings and in researching how best to preserve and restore them. The conservation of a major artwork can take months, cost thousands of dollars, and be a dramatic story in itself. No wonder that many conservation projects have been sources of intense public interest.

Oil paintings can be remarkably durable, although their structure is complex and delicate. Painting a picture in oil means practicing a craft side-by-side with art. Usually paintings are built in several layers: sizing, a ground, several layers of paint, and sometimes a coating of varnish, all applied to a canvas or wood support. Each of these components reacts to heat, light, moisture, and the aging process itself in a different way or at a different pace. Chemical and physical changes in the various components begin as soon as a painting is created and never really stop. Preserving the beauty of

How charming, yet precarious, to fill a home with a collection of paintings in this manner. Proper hanging and display are the keys to the health of a painting collection.

The display conditions of this nineteenth-century portrait allowed a heavy grime layer to accumulate. Here it is shown half cleaned.

a painting and prolonging its life does not mean arresting the aging process because that is impossible. Fortunately, not all the effects of aging are harmful. Mild cracking and darkening are part of the natural aging process and are usually accepted as such. The more serious darkening or yellowing that stems from grime or the long-term discoloring of the varnish and which obscures the artist's intention, can be addressed by a professional conservator. To preserve a painting, however, it is also essential to stabilize the tendency of the component layers, each made of a different material, to deteriorate or separate from each other as they age.

Keeping Your Paintings Healthy

The principal threat to oil paintings is structural damage, especially damage that causes the layers of the painting to separate from each other or the support. The artist's selection of materials or use of experimental techniques makes some paintings especially unstable. Damage to paintings is commonly caused in several ways. Temperature and relative-humidity extremes, or fluctuations, make the picture's components expand or contract at different rates, causing them to break up. The result may be lifting or flaking paint. Improper handling or mounting is another source of many problems. Paintings may distort, be punctured, or warp because of poor framing, hanging, or handling. A bad job of cleaning or restoration also can cause serious, irreversible damage to paintings.

Paintings thrive in a climate similar to that in which people are comfortable. Excessive heat and relative humidity may cause sagging or tightening of the canvas or distortion of the support. Keep the relative humidity in rooms where paintings are hung at around 50 percent. Higher relative humidity may cause a whitish cloudy bloom in the varnish of the painting. Dampness can make the paint tacky, and it also increases the likelihood of mold growth. A cold, dry climate, on the other hand, makes paint brittle and more likely to crack or flake.

Clearly, attics and basements are no place for paintings. The place of honor over a working fireplace is not good either, since it is likely to become very hot and dry there. In fact, pictures should not be hung near any heat or air conditioning source or air vent where pollution may flow. Incandescent lights generate heat that can damage paintings, and direct sunlight is also harmful. A picture can be effectively illuminated with cool fiberoptic picture lights or overhead lighting placed at a distance that will protect the surface from heat. Finally, it is important to keep foreign objects off paintings and their frames. That particularly includes plants. It is not a good idea to decorate a painting with greens or place a picture among flowers or plants.

Because paintings are more fragile than they seem, they should be handled with special care. It is important to attach a cardboard backing behind the reverse of the painting to protect it. Paintings should be hung from two mounting points, with _mirror-plate_ hangers or _D-rings_ rather than screw eyes attached to the frame. This technique provides maximum stability. The wall mountings should also be two mirror hangers. Individual nails or self-adhesive hooks are much more likely to fail, letting a painting drop to the floor, sometimes with truly disastrous results. For a smaller, lightweight painting, twisted multistrand picture wire attached securely to D-rings on the painting's frame and hung from a solid wall mount may be adequate.

Use special care when moving or storing paintings. Be sure to have at least two people to support and place a picture when it is being moved or hung.

To store a painting, trim clean pieces of cardboard equal to the largest dimension of the frame and place them over the front and back of the picture. Wrap the painting in paper, label it, and place it upright against a wall, supported with blocks of packing foam so it will not slip. If possible, store paintings against the wall of a dark, little-used closet or in a vacant room, well out of the way of foot traffic. Stored paintings should be elevated several inches above floor level to protect from leaks or floods. Above all, keep paintings in a place with a controlled climate.

Top:
The damage to this portrait is a result of being stored unprotected in an attic.

Above:
This detail shows heat blisters caused by a light bulb.

The back of a framed painting with (1) padded rabbet, (2) backing board attached to stretcher with screws and washers, (3) D-rings to hang painting, (4) brass mending plates screwed into frame to secure the painting, and (5) rubber spacers for air circulation

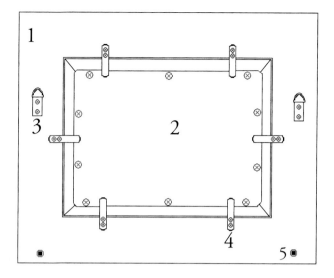

Cleaning or repairing a painting is part science, part craft; it is a job for a trained professional. The only cleaning a painting and its frame should receive in the home is a light dusting with a very soft, clean, dry brush. First, inspect the picture using a flashlight held at an oblique angle to better illuminate cracks or lifting paint. If it is cracking or flaking, don't even dust it, as you might cause flakes to detach. If the surface is intact, start at the top and gently brush downward. To make sure the brush you use remains clean, keep it in its own bag and don't use it for any other purpose. Cloths, feather dusters, or lambswool dusters should not be used on paintings because they can catch on raised areas. Never use any kind of cleaning agent, wax, oil, or polish. If you have a painting protected with

Above:
These washboard deformations and cracks were caused by improper storage of an oil on canvas rolled face inward.

Right:
The tissue placed over this painting was a misguided attempt to protect it during a household move. The tissue actually came in contact with and adhered to the surface of the painting.

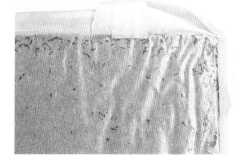

glass that needs to be cleaned, apply glass cleaner sparingly to a rag, then clean the glazing. Don't spray glass cleaner directly on the glazing as it could run into the frame and damage the picture.

Incidentally, even if you decide to have a painting restored, it is often best to keep the present frame, particularly if it may be the original. The frame can add to the value of a painting if it is itself an antique and enhances the historic context of the picture. Even if you change the frame, be sure to retain and label the frame that came to you with the picture.

Caring for Your Paintings: A Checklist

✓ Hang paintings away from sources of heat, airborne pollutants, and direct sunlight
✓ Don't store paintings in attics or basements
✓ Illuminate paintings with cool fiber-optic picture lights or overhead lighting at a safe distance that will not heat the surface
✓ Hang pictures from two mounting points, securing mirror-plate hangers to the frame
✓ Use picture or mirror hangers on the wall, not individual nails or self-adhesive hooks
✓ Inspect the surface of your paintings for cracks or flaking
✓ Dust pictures that are not cracked or flaking, and frames from the top down with a soft, clean, dry brush used only for this purpose; don't use cloths or dusters
✓ Never use cleaning agents, sprays, waxes, polishes, or oils on paintings
✓ If a picture is reframed, label and keep the original frame

Fabrics

I . . . chose my wife, as she did her wedding gown, not for a fine glossy surface, but for such qualities as would wear well.

—Oliver Goldsmith, *The Vicar of Wakefield*

Many families own needlework in the form of samplers that are treasured for their beauty and craftsmanship.

Clothing and textiles add color to life. For many reasons, they are among our most cherished family treasures. Quilts, samplers, and baby clothes are precious, not just for their intrinsic value, but also because of who made them, how they were made, and who wore them. Our ancestors created many of these articles in a now-extinct social context—sewing circles, quilting parties, and the like. These heirlooms can tell us a good deal about our own family history as well as the social fabric of times past.

Other textiles, such as a military uniform, a lace table-cloth, an ethnic rug, or a rag doll, can also have special meaning for a family, regardless of who made them. Proper care of any fabric will make a significant difference in its useful life. Long after a brightly colored shawl is worn or an embroidered handkerchief is carried, it can be admired for its beauty and craftsmanship and treasured as a link to the family's past. We handle textiles so much we become familiar with them and perhaps grow more care-less than when we handle other valuable objects. Preserving these heirlooms in good condition for occasional display, or even rare use, takes just a little extra care.

Scientific dating of woven artifacts discovered within the last decade has changed our understanding of the history of manufactured fabrics to a stunning degree. We know now that people have been manufacturing sophisticated woven fabrics for more than twenty thousand years. That was long before they were smelting ores to make the weapons and tools we have used to classify prehistoric epochs. Cloth made of spun and woven fibers—cotton, flax, silk, or wool—can last a long time, though it can also be very fragile.

Textiles deteriorate as the result of chemical changes, mechanical wear, or mishandling. The energy from light, especially sunlight, does the most to speed deterioration. It makes colors fade and breaks down textile fibers. It also affects finishes such as starch, inducing discoloration. High temperature has a similar, though somewhat slower, effect. High or low relative humidity, and rapid changes in relative humidity, are other hazards. High relative humidity can lead to mold or mildew, very low relative humidity to drying out and crumbling. Rapid changes in relative humidity cause fibers to break down, or if there is more than one material in an object, differing rates of shrinkage and swelling will cause the components to separate.

Fabrics are also harmed by dirt, grit, and chemicals. Chemical damage comes from atmospheric pollution, exposure to the acid in

Fabrics can be a record of family history. Note the monograms stitched into the front of this christening gown.

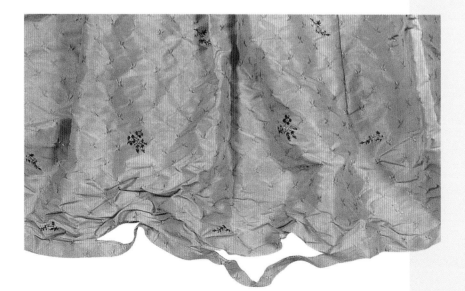

This detail of a dress exhibits damage from exposure to light. Note both the fading and deterioration of fibers.

Opposite:
The quilts we are so fond of preserving are not only beautiful to look at but also remind us of the social setting in which they were created.

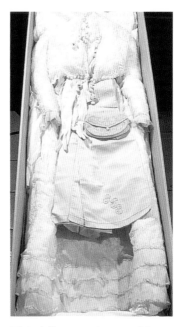

This delicate antique wedding dress and accessories are optimally stored together in a box that provides support and protection.

paper or wood that comes in contact with the fabric, and harsh cleaners such as bleach and ammonia.

Finally, fabrics are damaged by stress from handling or even storing, especially as they grow older and become more fragile. For example, a wedding dress hanging vertically will gradually be distorted in shape or even pulled apart by its own weight. The folds in a flag will become creases that cannot be removed after long periods of storage.

Keeping Fabrics Strong, Clean, and Bright

You can protect textiles best by minimizing their exposure to light, especially light from the sun or a fluorescent tube. Keeping items carefully stored in a drawer or a dark closet is best for their long-term survival, but that also takes much of the pleasure out of owning them.

When a large item such as a quilt is displayed, or even when it is stored, it should be laid flat or hung at an angle with enough support to make sure the top part is not torn or stretched. Costumes or clothing should rest on a plastic (not wood) hanger padded with unbleached cotton cloth. The hanger should fit the shoulders of the garment; it should be sufficiently padded to protect the shape, as well as long enough to extend to the shoulder seam, but no farther. Don't hang knit, bias-cut, or very heavy garments that will stretch or rip. Conservators recommend that people wear clean white cotton gloves when handling antique textiles. They also recommend that you carry fragile textiles in their boxes or on a tray, rather than holding them in your hands or draping them over your arm.

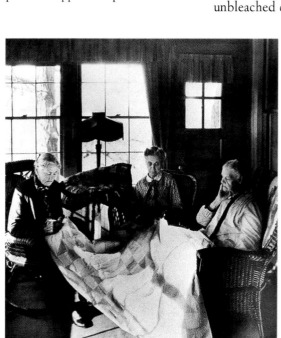

Preserving fabric objects that were made for functional purposes necessitates some trade-offs. Continued use and cleaning of textiles hastens their deterioration. The wise owner weighs the object's functional value against its antique or sentimental value, and chooses whether to use the object or keep it for display. A compromise—use on rare, special occasions—is also possible. You may, for instance, display a Civil War uniform for a short period of time in a dimly lighted room with no great harm.

You might decide it is worth the risk to let your cousin wear your wedding dress or to lend your grandmother's christening gown to a friend on rare occasions. But if a garment is precious to you, such uses should be kept to a minimum and great care should be taken. Wearing should be restricted to someone the same size or smaller than the person who originally wore the garment. The borrower should be careful to avoid exposing the garment to makeup and antiperspirants, in addition to other normal hazards. Very precious and fragile antique clothing such as an antebellum ball gown should not be dry cleaned, bleached, or even washed; therefore, soiling that arises from wearing it cannot be repaired. Spills, of course, should be blotted up immediately. Ironing or steaming may set the soils. Limits on cleaning or washing newer textile treasures may not be so strict. When in doubt about what to do, consult a conservator.

This padded hanger provides proper support for storage of a garment.

Even storage has its hazards. Because the acid found in wood and many papers can harm them, textiles should be stored in boxes made of acid-free materials, with layers separated by unbuffered tissue paper. Alternatively, they can be wrapped in clean white sheets. To avoid making creases in a piece that must be folded, the folds can be padded with crumpled rolls of unbuffered tissue. Since pesticides or mothballs should not be used to protect stored fabrics, it is very important that they be inspected frequently and the best house-

Acid-free padding used with fabrics boxed for storage prevents creases in the material and protects delicate decorative elements.

This textile is being rolled onto a tube for storage. For a large textile, choose an acid-free tube at least three inches in diameter. Place the textile on top of a piece of unbleached pre-washed muslin that is several inches larger than the textile. Slowly roll the textile onto the tube, ensuring that no wrinkles or snags are created. To hold the textile onto the tube, use 3- to 5-inch sections of acid-free mat board wrapped around the tube and secured with cotton-twill tape.

keeping practices followed. To store rugs or heavy blankets, roll them with the pile outward and wrap them in washed muslin (undyed cotton) or a white sheet. It's never wise to store heirloom textiles in attics or basements because extremes and fluctuations in temperature and relative humidity are so harmful to them.

As already noted, very old and very valuable textiles should not be washed or dry cleaned. The only way to safely clean sturdy heirloom fabrics with no loose beads or threads is with the circular brush attachment of the vacuum cleaner, with the cleaner set on low suction. A clean piece of cotton cheesecloth should be wrapped over the attachment. Vacuum by patting the surface as if you were blotting it gently and systematically.

Caring for Your Fabric Treasures: A Checklist

✓ Keep fabrics out of sun and fluorescent light as much as possible; limit display time
✓ Keep fabrics where temperatures and relative humidity are moderate, not in basements or attics
✓ Blot spills immediately; never wash or dry clean fragile antique textiles
✓ Don't use makeup or antiperspirants when wearing clothing too fragile and valuable to be dry-cleaned
✓ Store folded textiles in acid-free boxes with unbuffered tissue or white sheeting between layers
✓ Inspect stored fabrics frequently; do not use pesticides or mothballs
✓ Display material flat or hung at an angle to reduce pull
✓ Support costumes on a well-padded plastic hanger that is as wide as the garment's shoulders
✓ Sturdy fabrics can be cleaned by vacuuming on low suction with the brush attachment covered with cotton cheesecloth

What a touching tribute for a modern bride to wear her mother's or grandmother's wedding dress. This bride (*right*) found her mother's gown (*left*) in a black, plastic garbage bag where it had been stored for thirty years. The dress had yellowed and needed some treatment to stabilize the silk veil. After her wedding, the daughter had the dress cleaned and is now storing it in an acid-free box with acid-free tissue to ensure it survives and can be worn by someone in the next generation.

PRESERVING A NEW WEDDING DRESS

A brand new wedding dress is a good candidate for preservation. By taking steps to protect it immediately after the wedding, you can ensure it will look better and hold up longer. There are commercial services that will prepare your wedding dress for storage, and at least one that offers free online advice on how you can do it yourself. Among the important things to remember: wash your gown (or have it cleaned, depending on the material) immediately after the wedding; don't use starch, conditioning agents, or finishing chemicals. Store the gown without making creases (using a pure batting material to fill in folds) covered with unbuffered tissue paper in an acid-free box. Make sure the box is large enough to accommodate the dress with a minimum of folds. Kits are made for this purpose, but be careful to choose one with acid-free materials.

Furniture

Learn the lines and don't bump into the furniture.

—Attributed to Noel Coward

It is a special privilege to inherit antique furniture whose beauty can grace a home.

Furniture fills many functions and comes in many styles—utilitarian, formal and traditional, warm and comfortable, exotic or eclectic. Wood is a major component of most furniture, but the wood is often partially covered with paint or varnish and textile or leather upholstery. Most furniture also has metal fasteners, and many pieces have metal decorations. Some modern furniture is made of metal, glass, or synthetics. People sit on furniture, and place things upon it as well—from bowls of flowers in water to burning candles. The intricacy of furniture construction plus the numerous functions furniture must perform can make its proper care more complicated than the care of other heirlooms.

Millions of Americans are interested in old furniture, and if the viewership of the *Antiques Roadshow* on public television is a clue, that number is increasing. Many families have at least some furniture handed down from parents, grandparents, or more remote ancestors. A fortunate few possess examples of the American craftsmanship that first emerged in the late eighteenth and early nineteenth centuries, or the costly furniture imported from Europe—mainly Britain—during the same period. Some families acquire antiques or buy new furniture with an eye to the future. They plan to make these furnishings part of the heritage they will pass along to their children or grandchildren. Whether a family's furniture is already old or brand new, if it is of good quality, proper care will go a long way toward assuring its place in a family's heritage.

Some old furniture is too fragile and too valuable for everyday use. Identify pieces in that category, enlisting the help of a conservator or professional appraiser if there is any doubt. Using delicate pieces risks their destruction—by an innocent visitor, for example. Storing them under improper conditions means slower but equally certain destruction. Delicate, valuable pieces should be displayed with the kind of protection museums provide. If that is not possible, you might consider donating your piece to a museum. However, most family heirloom furniture is not museum quality and, with sensible use, can be displayed and enjoyed for years.

Keeping Your Furniture Strong and Beautiful

Many conservators observe that people are the main threat to furniture; pets also cause a great deal of harm. Some damage comes from destructive or careless handling and some from poorly conceived or performed restorations. People damage furniture with burning cigarettes, liquid spills, and harmful cleaning products. They also lift chairs by their arms and drag rather than lift tables to move them, causing parts to loosen. Improper restoration includes using the wrong materials and techniques—paints and adhesives, for example. Poor restoration strategies are also a problem: original components are removed accidentally, original surfaces are sanded, or elements are replaced inappropriately.

The environment is the second leading threat to furniture. Principal environmental hazards are temperature, humidity, and light. Wide and frequent fluctuations in temperature and relative humidity cause wood to warp and split and joints to separate. High temperature and relative humidity also hasten the degradation of upholstery and wood. Exposure to light, especially sunlight, causes fading and also hastens deterioration.

The basic care of furniture is relatively simple. Regular light dusting with a magnetic dust cloth is the best practice. Commercial oils that claim to "feed" the wood or other finish, or sprays containing silicone, should not be used. They do more harm than good over the

Below:
This ball and claw foot has been scarred by a vacuum cleaner.

Bottom:
Antique furniture is a functional and beautiful way to integrate family history with present-day living. Exposure to sunlight, however, is one of the primary hazards for furniture.

Polishing the brass hardware on this desk has damaged the surrounding wood finish.

long run and their effects, notably discoloration, are impossible to remove. If necessary, clean surfaces with a lint-free cloth lightly dampened with water. You can use paste wax sparingly once a year on wooden parts to make them easier to dust. It is important to avoid applying the wax to unfinished or damaged areas, since it is likely to collect in such areas and discolor them even further.

Upholstery can be vacuumed carefully on low suction with the brush attachment wrapped in clean cotton cheesecloth. Vacuum by gently and systematically patting the surface as if you were blotting it. It is best to avoid stain-resisting or waterproofing chemical treatments on antique textiles.

Careful handling is another key to keeping your furniture in good shape. Heavy or sharp objects that rest on furniture should be padded on the bottom with felt to avoid scratching the surface. Keep water, alcohol, food, grease, and candles away from furniture you value, unless the furniture, such as a dining table, is covered by appropriate padding. Cut flowers or plants that drop pollen can also damage finishes. When there are spills, move swiftly to sop up liquids; quick action reduces the risk of damage or stains.

Move furniture as little as possible and be especially reluctant to move fragile or damaged pieces. When moving is necessary, give thoughtful planning and attention to how you do it. Make sure

This tabletop shows water damage from fresh flower arrangements. If you display fresh flowers, place a pad under the vase to protect furniture from condensation droplets, petals, and pollen. Furniture makes an expensive coaster.

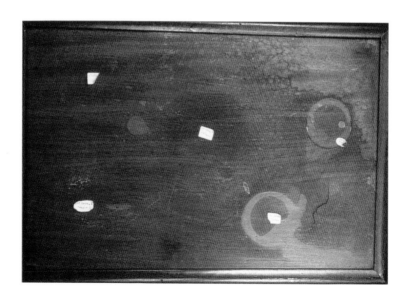

there are sufficient movers and that they work slowly, gripping furniture with both hands below the center of gravity and at balance points. Don't lift tables by their tops; many tabletops are attached only with dowels. Use dollies for heavy pieces. Never allow furniture to be dragged across the floor.

Keep your furniture healthy by keeping it in rooms with stable relative humidity and temperature. The temperature should be around 72 degrees Fahrenheit and the relative humidity about 50 percent. Since wood absorbs water from the atmosphere, rapid changes in relative humidity cause it to warp, swell unevenly, and crack. This is especially true of veneers. Relative humidity above 65 percent hastens the deterioration of wood. More serious perhaps, high temperature and relative humidity encourage the growth of mold and fungi, as well as the rapid reproduction of insect pests that infest and damage wooden objects. Very low relative humidity causes wood to dry out and crack. Fluctuations in temperature alone usually don't harm wood very much directly, but wooden furniture often has metal fasteners and attachments. Changes in temperature cause the wood and metal to expand at different rates. After several episodes of uneven expansion and contraction, metal pieces are likely to be loosened.

Basements and attics are especially subject to temperature and relative humidity extremes. Storing furniture in such out-of-the-way places makes it harder to detect the growth of mold, mildew, rodent damage, or insect infestations. Find a place for valuable pieces in large closets or spare rooms. Likewise, because of the harmful properties of light, limit exposure to direct sunlight or even to constant artificial light sources. Windows with glass treated to filter ultraviolet light or with ultraviolet-filtering film will protect furniture.

The value of antique furniture—for purposes of family history, culture, and even monetary appraisal—depends largely on how much of the original structure, finish, and upholstery remain intact. The more the better. Although refinishing and reupholstering can make furniture look newer and superficially more attractive, removing or altering anything that was original—finish, upholstery, hardware—diminishes the value of the piece as an antique. Stripping finishes on fine furniture, or even removing the rings caused by a cold beverage glass, should not be undertaken except with the advice of a conservator.

This chair has been severely damaged by powderpost beetles. Routine inspections will help prevent bug infestations from developing into major problems. Be sure to also inspect hidden areas such as inside drawers.

Caring for Your Furniture: A Checklist

✓ Use paste wax sparingly once a year to make dusting easier; avoid waxing damaged areas

✓ Don't use silicone sprays or oils that claim to "feed" surfaces

✓ Clean upholstery by vacuuming with the brush attachment wrapped in cotton cheesecloth; avoid stain-resistant treatments

✓ Pad the bases of objects placed on valuable furniture and protect surfaces from spills

✓ Always move furniture slowly, with care and attention to detail

✓ Keep furniture out of direct sunlight and away from hot spotlights and lamps

✓ Keep furniture away from temperature or relative humidity extremes, and especially out of basements and attics

✓ Check regularly for damage from insects and mold

✓ Don't remove original finish or upholstery from antique pieces

Leather upholstery is more sensitive to light than wooden furniture components and shows damage sooner. When possible, it is best to keep original upholstery intact.

Clocks and Watches

I wasted time, and now doth time waste me;
For now hath time made me his numbering clock;
My thoughts are minutes.

—William Shakespeare, *Richard II*

Grandfather clocks, mantel clocks, commemorative pocket watches—timepieces are among the most common of our prized family treasures. A clock may be a piece of furniture, art object, or functional device. However it came into the family and whatever its current use, an heirloom timepiece can be both attractive and serviceable.

Clocks can have elements that are works of art. This painted nineteenth-century American clock dial was removed and treated by a professional paintings conservator.

There are many types and variations of old clocks and watches—tall clocks, wall clocks, observatory regulators, miniature portable clocks, and very precise naval chronometers, as well as elegant pocket and wrist watches. Clocks are made of a multitude of materials—copper, brass, steel, silver, gold, lead, zinc, wood, fabric, leather, and shell or bone. Clocks can provide more information than merely the time and date; some tell the lunar day of the month or the tides.

Some well-built clocks are still keeping very good time after six hundred years. Such endurance won't happen to your clock by luck, however. Clocks face numerous perils. The greatest hazards are: time itself, the inevitable slow wearing away of the mechanism; environmental damage, mostly from high temperature and relative humidity, and airborne pollutants; sunlight; poor maintenance, handling, and human intervention.

Keeping Your Antique Clocks Ticking

The components of a clock's mechanism gradually wear away from the friction of their own operation. This may happen slowly or with distressing speed. Properly scheduled professional lubrication and maintenance can have a major impact on the clock or watch's usable life. Under ideal environmental conditions, a clock or watch should be oiled once every three years and fully dismantled and cleaned once every eight to ten years. When the environment is less than ideal—polluted or very humid, for example—a clock will need more frequent cleaning. Although lubricants reduce friction, they also attract airborne abrasives, which, in combination with the fine metallic particles produced by wear, make an abrasive slurry that must be removed at reasonable intervals. Lubricants also have finite lifetimes, usually three to five years.

Clock maintenance and repair are highly specialized skills, so take your heirloom timepiece to a trained professional for cleaning and lubricating. For help in finding such a person, you may need to rely on the experience of others. The conservation department at the nearest

The works of an old watch. Friction gradually wears on components of a timepiece's mechanism. Thus, an antique clock or watch should be oiled every three years and dismantled and cleaned by a professional once every eight to ten years.

museum is a good place to begin your search. When you find a candidate, it is appropriate to ask about his or her training and request references.

If your clock or watch has been idle for more than a year, or been in a flood or fire, you should have it examined and, if necessary, cleaned before it is operated again. Ultrasonic cleaning of clocks made prior to 1850 is not a good idea. It can be harmful to the hardened brass that is a principal component of old clocks. Ammoniated cleaning solutions and those that contain nitrogen should also be avoided.

Winding your clock properly is an important part of its care. Overwinding is harmful. It can break the mainspring, cable, or other components. Ask your professional repairer how to wind your particular clock and how long you should expect it to run between windings. Various clocks are designed to run continuously for periods of from four hundred days to only thirty hours. It is a good idea to fix a single day and time each week to wind all your clocks. Make only the number of half-turns of the winding key that will keep the clock functioning without overwinding. If you do not know and don't want to risk experimentation, a professional clock repairer can usually provide guidance. When you are winding, be sure that the key fits snugly in the square in the clock and that the works are not loose in the case.

Setting your clock properly is also important. Place your finger at the base, near the center—not at the tip—of the minute hand. Press it gently forward in the clockwise direction. Never force the hand; if you feel resistance, stop. Gently push the hand back about 3 minute marks, then press forward again. Some clocks allow separate hour and minute-hand settings, but unless you are certain yours does, don't try it. If you are setting a clock that strikes, it is normally necessary to keep the striking synchronized with the time by allowing the clock to strike at each of its normal striking points around the clock. For example, let the clock strike three times at three o'clock before proceeding further, the same at four, and so on until the proper time is reached. If the clock strikes on half- or quarter-hours, the same principle applies. If you have to move the clock eleven hours ahead, as in the fall when we return to standard time, it may be easier to shut the clock off for an hour.

It is a good idea to secure tall or wall clocks to a wall. They are especially vulnerable to vibrations and being displaced by acciden-

Tall clocks should be secured to a wall. Most already have holes in the backboard. Before moving a pendulum clock, either remove or secure the pendulum.

tal bumping or even the opening and closing of the doors for winding. In the case of tall clocks, the movement of the pendulum can set the weights swinging sympathetically. That will cause the case to sway imperceptibly, which can affect timing or even cause the clock to stop intermittently. Continuous minute rocking may also crack the glue in the case and loosen joints. Most tall clocks already have

Proper winding is key to the long-term health of antique clocks.

several holes in the backboard, so it is not necessary to drill new ones. Wall clocks should be secured through the backboard close to the bottom of the clock case.

If you move a pendulum clock, even across the room, the pendulum should be removed or secured in place. Don't use adhesive tape, because its chemicals are damaging, and the tape may pull away part of the finish of the clock when it is removed. If your clock is powered by weights, let it run down fully and then remove the weights from the case. If you are moving a great distance, it is a good idea to have a professional clock repairer pack your clock for the move and another unpack and install the clock in its new home.

Clocks need a clean environment with a steady temperature no more than 72 degrees Fahrenheit and relative humidity around 50 percent. This is particularly important for the functioning of a longcase wooden clock as well as for the security of its case. Don't put your clock near heating and air-conditioning vents since that increases the chance of harm from airborne contaminants, as well as from frequent temperature changes.

Most antique clocks should be cleaned on the outside only by gentle dusting with a clean brush. If there is intricate carving or loose veneer, an artist's bristle brush may be used. Do not use furniture oils on clock cases or polish metal parts. See chapters on furniture (page 79) and metal objects (page 96) for further guidance on the proper care of your clock case. Never try to clean clock dials with detergents or solvents of any kind.

Do not dismantle or try to repair an antique clock or watch on your own. Make sure repairs are done by an expert, and insist on the most conservative repairs consistent with safe functioning, even if they are more expensive. That is, keep as much of the original time-piece as possible. If part of a component is damaged, have only that part repaired or replaced, not the whole component. If a new part must be made for the clock, keep the old piece with the clock along with clear documentation of the repair. In terms of the monetary value of the clock or watch, you will be more than repaid for the conservative approach.

Caring for Your Clocks: A Checklist

- ✓ Have your heirloom clock oiled every three years and cleaned every eight to ten years by a trained professional
- ✓ Do not start a damaged watch or clock, or one that has been stopped for more than a year, without having it first checked by a professional
- ✓ Ultrasonic cleaning is not good for clocks made before 1850
- ✓ Clocks and watches should not be wound more than necessary
- ✓ Set clocks by pressing the tip of your finger against the center of the minute hand; move the hand in a clockwise direction, but do not force it
- ✓ When you reset a striking clock, allow the clock to strike at each normal point as you move the hand forward
- ✓ Secure your tall or wall clock to a wall or firm surface
- ✓ Keep clocks in rooms with relative humidity around 50 percent and moderate temperature
- ✓ Dust clocks carefully with a soft brush; never wash or use solvents on the dial
- ✓ Properly prepare clocks before moving them; always secure a pendulum before moving
- ✓ Let no one but a professional repair your old clock, and retain as much of the original clock intact as possible

Ceramics and Glass

Glass and ceramics can be functional or art forms. This plate was probably never intended for use at the table. Today, the central image of San Francisco's Golden Gate before the bridge gives the plate historical interest. Careful display will minimize the risk of damage from falling or being bumped.

Fortune is like glass—the brighter the glitter, the more easily broken.

—Publilius Syrus, Maxim 280

Dishes, pots, and statues made of clay—*ceramics*—are among the oldest of human creations as well as the most beautiful. Stemware and other fine pieces made of glass have long been cherished for their delicacy and elegance. Some of these objects are passed down in families for sentimental reasons or because they are splendid art of significant monetary value. But many ceramic and glass family treasures are functional. Dishes, from pottery to the best china, along with crystal, often come into the family as wedding presents. Thus, they are part of a family's history from the very outset. Dishes and crystal, like silverware, are central props in family ceremonies. They are tokens of the mood and importance of an occasion; the "good" china and crystal bring beauty and dignity to a family gathering, and they honor special guests. With proper care, decorative plates, figurines, bowls, vases, and pots, as well as sets of china and crystal, can be preserved for many years in excellent condition.

FAMILY HOLIDAYS—FAMILY TREASURES

Holidays are important for families. They are milestones of the year as well as of the family's march in the parade of generations. They are the occasions for gatherings, feasts, and celebrations. The good china, linen, and silver come out and, often, so does the family album. The nature of family holidays creates a special opportunity for stewardship of family treasures as well as some special risks to fragile objects.

One of the themes of this book is the importance of periodic examinations of the beautiful and precious, but also vulnerable, objects that families treasure. The approach of a family holiday is a good time to take a look at how your trea-

Holiday gatherings are an occasion to bring out the family china and crystal. Their use at these celebrations also risks damage.

Though Kwanza is a relatively new holiday, it is establishing traditions with objects that will be used annually during family celebrations and passed down to future generations.

sures are displayed or stored. How are they faring? Do they need to be reorganized, sorted, documented, dusted, or better stored?

Family gatherings create another kind of opportunity as well. They are a good time for you to compare notes with other people in the family, especially the older people, on the provenance of family treasures. Who made this quilt? When? Under what circumstances? Who else has owned and used it? Holiday gatherings are an ideal time to make a written record. This is especially true of the family photograph album. Who are all of those people? Where were those pictures taken? As your treasures brighten holiday celebrations, holidays can enrich the heritage surrounding family treasures.

About Ceramics and Glass

Ceramic material ranges from delicate, almost translucent porcelain to the bricks used to build a house. The differences in ceramics depend mainly on whether the clay used is *soft-* or *hard-bodied*, its color, the temperature at which it is fired, and the *glaze*, if any, that was applied to seal and decorate the object. Unfired or underfired clay objects, such as *adobe*, tend to be unstable and absorb water. *Earthenware* is fired at temperatures high enough to make it water insoluble, but it remains porous unless it is glazed. *Glazing* involves covering the object with a coating of glass through a reheating process, but the coating does not actually combine chemically with the clay. Various glazing techniques produce striking variations in the finish of ceramic objects, but some techniques make the objects more porous and subject to staining, cracking, and chipping. Porcelain and *stoneware* are fired mostly at very high temperatures, making them nonporous and quite brittle. Unglazed porcelain is called *bisque*.

Glass is made mostly of silica from sand, alkali, and calcium. It may be combined with various metal oxides to produce different effects. Crystal, for example, contains a significant amount of lead, enough to activate the metal detector at an airport. The lead makes the resultant glass heavy, very clear, and soft—ideal for cutting. The glassmaking process is similar to the process of fabricating

Ceramics range from low-fired earthenware (*above*) that is porous and highly susceptible to water damage to high-fired porcelain (*top*) that is relatively impervious to water.

The staining in this ceramic was caused by water penetration through a crack in the glaze.

metals, but the resulting molecular structure of glass is different.

Because they are made of minerals, ceramics and glass are little harmed, as a rule, by moderate doses of environmental stresses such as temperature, high relative humidity, and light. There are some exceptions, however, which will be described in the following section. The primary threat to ceramics and glass is breakage from human handling or other accidents. One conservator lists the leading occasions for breakage as washing; shipping or moving without proper packing; dropping (often by a child); or being knocked off a shelf by dusting, a cat, or a curtain blown by wind. Objects can also be stained or broken as the result of improper storage or rapid extreme temperature changes.

A great deal of unnecessary damage is also done by poor repairs. Gluing a treasured broken bowl back together is a job for an expert. To help the expert, be sure to collect as many of the pieces as possible, including the smallest fragments. Wrap the pieces in separate paper towels so that the fragments will not rub against each other, causing further deterioration.

Sometimes prized ceramics are broken. In that unfortunate event, collect all the fragments and wrap them individually in tissue to prevent further damage. Repair is best left to a professional, since common household adhesives can discolor and further fracture delicate ceramics.

Safeguarding Family Treasures of Ceramic and Glass

Careful, patient handling is the most important thing you can do to keep ceramics and glass treasures in good shape. China and crystal give the most pleasure when used for the purpose for which they were designed—as serving pieces at festive occasions—but antique ceramics should not be used for cooking or warming food. In fact, they should never be heated much above room temperature, or exposed to sudden temperature shocks such as that caused by pouring hot water into a cold bowl, for example.

After use, ceramic dishes and crystal should be hand washed individually in warm water with mild dishwashing soap, carefully and completely rinsed, and dried by hand with a soft towel. Washing is a vulnerable time for china and crystal. Be careful. It is a good idea to place a rubber or foam pad at the bottom of the sink when you are washing delicate pieces. Never wash unglazed ceramics; they are likely to absorb moisture and stain or soften and break. Never put valuable ceramics in a dishwasher, especially objects with gold trim, since it will quickly disappear.

You probably will decide some dishes and glassware are too valuable or too fragile to use at the table. For such purely decorative objects, dusting occasionally with a magnetic cloth is better than washing. It is best not to use sprays, polishes, or commercial cleaners on ceramics and glass, for several reasons. They can discolor, damage finishes, and make objects more difficult to handle safely. If dusting is insufficient and washing with mild detergent inappropriate, as in the case of hand-painted, unglazed, or repaired objects, use a brush with soft bristles or a gentle vacuum with a brush attachment. It is always safest to handle one object at a time with clean, dry hands.

People sometimes use very precious crystal or china for purposes that seem safer than service at the table. Some of these uses are indeed harmless, but others have risks. Live flower arrangements, colored water, and food storage in ceramic or glass objects are risky because they cause stains. It is best to avoid such uses of valuable pieces. If you have an important reason to use an object this way, try to find a watertight liner to protect it.

In order to minimize the need to clean, it is best to display antique objects in a case with a glass door. Such cases should not be in direct sunlight, which can cause designs to fade, or in places of extreme heat or cold. Cases or shelves should be level and not crowded; crowding increases the risk that a dust cloth will topple a figurine or cause one vase to fall on others.

When you store ceramics or glass objects, do not stack or allow the pieces to rest against each other. It is appropriate to stack plates, of course, if they are separated by paper toweling, flannel cloth, or thin layers of polyethylene, the same materials in which objects should be wrapped individually if they are to be moved. Though commonly used, newspaper, or even clean newsprint, is not good packing material for storing or moving glass or ceramic objects. It is a good idea to line a ground-glass bottle stopper with a thin layer of polyethylene film before putting it in the bottle.

Caring for Your Ceramics and Glass: A Checklist

Because these antique Christmas ornaments are displayed for a relatively short time once a year, special consideration of their storage conditions will keep them looking their best.

✓ Handle objects carefully, one at a time, with clean, dry hands

✓ Wash glazed and glass objects by hand; don't use a dishwasher

✓ It is best not to wash *unglazed* ceramics or those with gold edging, hand-painted decorations, or repairs

✓ Avoid dusting sprays, polishes, or commercial cleaners for glass and ceramics

✓ Display antique objects in a cabinet with glass doors if possible

✓ Display objects on level shelves, out of bright sunlight, in moderate temperatures

✓ Don't heat ceramics much above room temperature; be careful of exposing warm items to things that are cold or vice versa

✓ Don't store items in direct contact with other items; separate plates, and wrap each item separately for packing

✓ Use paper toweling, flannel, or a thin layer of polyethylene to wrap or separate objects; avoid newspaper or even clean newsprint

✓ Don't use heirloom glass or ceramics for food storage, live flower arrangements, or to hold colored water

✓ Collect all the pieces, including tiny fragments, of a broken object in separate paper towels; don't try to glue them together; take them to a professional

Silver, Other Decorative Metals, and Jewelry

The louder he talked of his honor, the faster we counted our spoons.

—Ralph Waldo Emerson, *Conduct of Life*

Silver is a noble metal. It is bright and lustrous, expensive enough to be a luxury but one within the financial reach of many families. Objects such as candlesticks, made of metal alloys like brass, also grace our homes and are passed down through generations. The appropriate care of different metals, however, even those with a similar appearance, often varies. Before you clean or polish an heirloom, be sure you know what it is made of.

Many treasured family objects are made of silver and other metals.

Silver

The family silver, especially if engraved with an ancestor's initials, is treasure with tradition. In some families, bringing out the silver by custom distinguishes certain holidays and symbolically seals particularly important occasions. The use of sterling lends ceremony to modern lives that usually are focused on convenience and efficiency. Objects of silver other than flatware and serving dishes—menorahs and cups, for example—also have ceremonial roles for some families. And collections of medals, coins, toilet articles, boxes, and other treasures are often prized for their intrinsic value and beauty.

Silver in its pure form is so unstable that it is rarely found in nature; it is extremely susceptible to combining with other minerals. The result is corrosion, the greatest threat to the survival of family treasures made of silver. Even when it is alloyed with another metal, as in bronze or brass, or a small amount of copper in utensils, silver is extremely susceptible to the form of corrosion called *tarnishing*. Tarnish is actually a black layer of silver sulfide, a combination of silver and gaseous sulfur from the atmosphere. Silver also combines easily with chlorides, oxygen, and hydroxides when it comes in contact with them. Even the minute traces of these elements found in the oil on human skin cause corrosion.

Each smear of tarnish consists of some atoms of the silver that have permanently detached themselves from the object to combine with sulfur. Removing discoloration by polishing removes even more of the underlying silver. Buffing does the same thing. Objects that have been polished or buffed repeatedly lose the sharpness of their shape—straight edges soften into curves—and their shine, since the alloyed metal corrodes away more slowly than the silver. Sadly, it is easy to polish through the coating layer of silver-plated objects, leaving a discolored and much diminished piece.

Because the leading cause of tarnish is the sulfur found in the air, silver objects that are used or displayed rather than carefully stored will inevitably acquire some tarnish. The earliest stage of corrosion, a light brown film, can be removed without polishing. If your piece has only minor tarnish, proceed with a gentle cleaning. Put a clean piece of flannel,

Too much polishing has dulled the detail of the silver pattern on the fork on the right.

Keeping the Sparkle in the Family Silver

muslin, or other soft cotton on the table as a work surface. If the piece is dirty, dust it lightly with a soft brush directed toward a vacuum nozzle. Select a broad brush with an all-wooden handle, or tape any metal parts so the brush handle will not scratch the silver. Do not use a dust cloth as it will not reach into small crevices, and it can scratch an object if it rubs trapped grit on the surface. Wash the piece in warm water with a mild detergent. Be sure not to immerse hollow-handled pieces or objects with crannies from which water cannot easily drain.

You should also hand wash silver that has been used to serve food as soon as the meal is finished. Dishwashers are risky for silver because they can cause pitting. Dry silver pieces thoroughly with a soft cloth immediately after they are washed. Use a dry corner of the same cloth to put the silverware and utensils in their containers without touching them. (Butlers in stately homes use clean cotton gloves.)

Using clean cotton gloves or a cloth to wipe off fingerprints when setting the table is also a good idea; the silver will look better and you can help prevent tarnish from fingerprints. Avoid exposing silver to acidic foods such as lemon and tomatoes, and to food such as eggs that contain sulfur. Fresh flowers, newspaper, rubber, wool, and salt are also harmful to your cherished silver. All of these things are powerful tarnishing agents.

Tarnish and corrosion make it necessary to clean and polish silver from time to time, but if you polish your silver pieces too often you

The silverplating on this Sheffield fused-plate tea urn has been worn away by polishing.

will destroy their crispness and beauty. Most commercial polishes and dips are too abrasive for the family silver and may contain damaging sulfuric acid or ammonia. Electrolytic, electrochemical, and aluminum with baking soda methods of removing tarnish are also harmful because they remove too much of the underlying silver.

Make sure the pieces are strong enough to withstand polishing. If you find cracks, weak areas, old repairs, and loose or missing parts, do not polish the piece yourself. Take it to a conservator.

How to Polish Silver

Also look for original organic surface coatings such as paint or shellac, which are sometimes applied to copper-alloy surfaces as part of the manufacturing process. *Patina* is another type of decorative and protective surface often applied to silver- or copper-alloy items. A patina is a thin chemically induced layer of relatively stable corrosion. Patina can also form over time from use and handling and can give an object the "patina of age." These organic surface layers and patina should not be removed by polishing.

You may need to remove old, waxy polish residues before you polish. Sometimes they can be removed by applying a few drops of mild detergent solution (for example, a 2 percent solution of Orvus® in water) to the spot, waiting a few minutes, and removing with cotton swabs. Be careful to avoid scratching the surface with the old polish and accumulated grime. Change swabs often and use a rolling rather than rubbing motion. If the residues cling, you can gently agitate them with a soft sable paintbrush, being careful to avoid scratching. Then rinse the piece thoroughly.

To polish silver (or copper alloys), mix in a shallow dish a small amount of precipitated calcium carbonate with a 2 percent solution of mild detergent and water. Do not substitute ground chalk or whiting for the precipitated calcium carbonate—they are abrasive and will scratch the object's surface. The mixture should be the consistency of cream.

Apply a small amount of the calcium carbonate mixture to the object with a piece of clean flannel or a wad of loose cotton, rubbing gently in a circular motion. Replace the cotton or flannel often as you work so that you are not merely grinding the removed tarnish and used calcium carbonate back into the surface. It takes very little calcium carbonate to polish an object—a common mistake is to use too much.

The tarnish on this silverplated tea set has been gently removed with a paste made from precipitated calcium carbonate and a mild detergent solution.

Once polishing has been completed, remove residues by rinsing the surface with cotton dipped in clean water. Dry the object thoroughly by wiping with a clean, dry, piece of flannel.

WHERE TO FIND SILVER-CARE MATERIALS

✓ Unbleached cotton flannel is available from fabric stores
✓ Orvus® detergent can be purchased from a veterinary supply house or a farm store
✓ Precipitated calcium carbonate is available from conservation suppliers
✓ Distilled or deionized water can be found at hardware and grocery stores
✓ Pacific Silver Cloth® is available from fine jewelers and conservation suppliers
✓ 3M AntiTarnish® Strips can be found in hardware stores and some supermarkets

Silver on display, like silver in use, may need to be polished from time to time; generally, however, it just should be dusted frequently. Dust actually attracts moisture and polluting chemicals from the air. Use a soft, dry brush that is set aside for that purpose only.

Displaying and Storing Your Silver

For storage, keep pieces individually wrapped in storage bags made of Pacific Silver Cloth®, or wrap them in sulfur- and acid-free tissue paper and seal in a polyethylene bag with a 3M AntiTarnish® Strip. Products such as these remove sulfur from the atmosphere, thereby minimizing tarnish and reducing the need for polishing. Don't store silver in plastic food bags or dry cleaner's bags. Silver should stored at a moderate temperature, in a place with low relative humidity, and away from the tarnishing agents mentioned above.

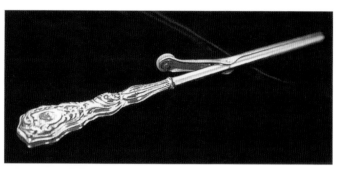

Even functional items such as this curling iron were once elegantly rendered in silver. Today this object is treasured for its uniqueness. When stored, it can be protected with a pollution scavenger that will inhibit the formation of tarnish.

Caring for Your Silver: A Checklist

✓ Keep agents of corrosion such as salt, acidic foods, newspaper, wool, and rubber away from silver vessels and utensils

✓ Wash silver pieces with warm water and mild soap; dry them thoroughly with a soft cloth

✓ Avoid electrolytic and electrochemical processes, as well as commercial polishes and dips

✓ Polish by gently applying a slurry of calcium carbonate and mild detergent

✓ After polishing, wash pieces with mild soap and water to remove residues and dry them well with a lint-free cloth

✓ After washing or polishing silver, handle it with a soft cloth or clean cotton gloves to prevent fingerprints

✓ Store pieces individually wrapped in storage bags made of Pacific Silver Cloth®, or wrapped in sulfur- and acid-free tissue paper and sealed in a bag with a 3M AntiTarnish® Strip

✓ Store silver at moderate temperature and relative humidity and away from agents of corrosion

Other Decorative Metals

Beautiful family heirlooms may be made of many metals not so noble as silver. Objects of bronze, brass, or copper have been passed down in families for generations. In addition, silver imitations like pewter, German silver (also called paktong), and argenta have been used to craft treasures of great monetary as well as sentimental value. Proper care of these objects varies, depending on the alloy of which they are made.

The first step in the proper treatment of any metal heirloom is to be certain exactly what metal the object is made of. This task can be tricky because many alloys have been created to simulate silver or gold and are difficult to distinguish. If you are not absolutely certain about a piece you are dealing with, it is a good idea to have the object examined and appraised by an expert—a conservator, a jeweler, or a reputable antique dealer.

Be very careful in handling plated metals because polishing will badly damage the finish on some silver-gilt, ormolu, and golden varnishes, virtually destroying their appearance. Gold-plating may be applied in such a thin layer that polishing will wear it away. Another hazard is the factory-applied lacquer or original patina on some brass, bronze, copper, and gold-plated objects. Excessive moisture or polishing may cause discoloration, blistering, or simply strip away part of the layer. These objects should be cleaned gently with a damp (not wet) cloth. Shiny brass and bronze can be treated exactly like silver—as described earlier in this chapter.

Pewter, German silver, and argenta should be dusted normally. If it is necessary, objects made of these alloys can be washed occasionally with mild soap and distilled water, then carefully dried.

Caring for Other Metals: A Checklist

✓ Polishing can destroy the surface of gold-plated, silver-gilt, ormolu, and golden varnishes

✓ Bronze, brass, copper, and gold-plated metal may have an original patina or factory-applied lacquer; wipe them carefully with a damp cloth

✓ Silver imitations like pewter, German silver, and argenta should be dusted and only occasionally washed and dried thoroughly

The family silver is not the only metal you may cherish. A wide range of objects made from other decorative metals, such as this brass button, may be treasured for many reasons, including historic value. This button was likely made at the time of George Washington's inauguration.

Coin collections bring a variety of metals together and can be a preservation challenge. The housing for this coin collection is poor because the acidic cardboard mounts will cause corrosion and the metal staples risk scratching. Ideally, coins should be stored in archival materials such as polyester sleeves, polyethylene zipper bags, or polystyrene or acrylic boxes.

Jewelry

*Kissing your hand may make you feel very, very good, but a
diamond and sapphire bracelet lasts forever.*

—Anita Loos, *Gentlemen Prefer Blondes*

Jewelry comes in various forms—rings, necklaces, earrings, brooches, pins, pendants, and combs among them—and may be made with various metals and alloys, which can be studded with precious and semiprecious stones or other material such as ivory or amber. A treasured piece of jewelry may be as simple as a gold band or as elaborate as a *cloisonné* pin. The principal use of jewelry is personal adornment, but it fills other roles. A queen's crown, the iron ring worn by a Roman citizen of the plebeian class, a general's stars, and a wedding band—all are examples of the use of jewelry to establish status. Heirloom jewelry passed down from a previous generation is a common focus of family pride.

Fine jewelry is typically composed of a variety of materials, many of which are more delicate than they seem. The main threat to jewelry is physical damage caused by normal wear or breakage. Rubies, emeralds, and sapphires are brittle and not nearly as hard as diamonds. They may be scratched by diamonds or even shatter if they receive a hard blow. Damage is also sometimes inflicted by

Caring for jewelry requires a knowledge not only of the characteristics of metals, but also of gemstones and other materials.

Often it is a surprise to learn how delicate and susceptible to damage gemstones can be. Opals are one such example; note how the stones in these antique rings have been chipped and cracked.

exposing delicate materials to harmful solvents or, in the case of porous stones or organic materials such as pearls, even water. And changes in fashion—the style of cutting diamonds, for example— can reduce the monetary if not the sentimental value of antique jewelry.

It is relatively easy to keep jewelry in good condition and looking its best. Certain precautions will help. It is a good idea to check

Keeping Your Jewelry Looking Its Best

jewelry with stones set in metal to make sure that no settings are loose. Even if you detect no problems, have jewelry with stones in exposed settings cleaned and checked by a reputable jeweler from time to time. Likewise, if you have strung pearls or beads, examine the string or wire for wear regularly and have the piece checked by a trusted professional. Strung beads or pearls should be restrung at intervals of five to seven years, especially if they are worn often.

Be careful cleaning jewelry. Many stones and organic material such as ivory can be harmed seriously by cleaning solvents. Never attempt to clean pearls by any method other than brushing gently with a clean brush. Opals, pearls, sapphires, turquoise, amber, coral, enamels, horn, tortoiseshell, and ivory should not be immersed in water. Foil-backed gems, paste, or rhinestones should not be immersed because the backing will deteriorate.

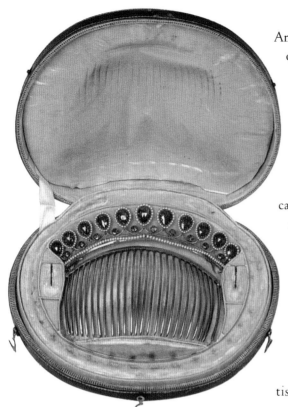

Individual pieces of jewelry should be stored separately to avoid abrasion.

Antique jewelry of these materials should be cleaned only by, or with the advice of, a conservator.

Jewelry without porous components and with settings that are open at the back—so that liquids will drain rather than collect—can be cleaned with soapy water in a dish lined with cloth or in a special jar with a mesh dripping basket. Allow the item to soak, then use a cotton swab or soft toothbrush to remove dirt from crevices. After the piece has dried, it can be buffed gently with a clean soft cloth. If the setting is closed, making it difficult to ensure that it will dry properly, the piece should not be immersed but brushed or swabbed gently with soapy water, then rinsed and dried in the same way.

Jewelry should be stored in individual lined compartments or individual bags or boxes to avoid the abrasions caused by contact with other jewelry. To avert possible harm to silver and some metal alloys as well as some softer minerals, use acid-free tissue as lining material.

Caring for Jewelry: A Checklist

✓ Check settings often to make sure no stones are loose
✓ Have jewelry cleaned and checked by a professional at regular intervals
✓ Have pearls and beads restrung every five to seven years, *before* the string breaks
✓ Don't clean with solvents or even wash semiprecious stones, organic material, or foil-backed gems, paste, or rhinestones used in jewelry
✓ Store antique jewelry in individual compartments, bags, or boxes; protect silver and soft minerals with acid-free, sulfur-free tissue paper

Special Collections

Musical Instruments

It is sweet to dance to violins
When Love and Life are fair:
To dance to flutes, to dance to lutes
Is delicate and rare:
But it is not sweet with nimble feet
To dance upon the air!

—Oscar Wilde, *The Ballad of Reading Gaol*

All of the world's cultures make music. The instruments of the music, though of broadly similar types, are as varied as the cultures themselves. In this multicultural nation, the whole panoply of musical instruments is found among families' treasures. Dozens of varieties of percussion, key-board, brasswind, woodwind, and stringed instruments are found in American homes. They represent many nations and every continent. Some are recently acquired by those rediscovering their roots; others have been

Sometimes family members may collect musical instruments.

This eighteenth-century flute survives in its original case. Even a small musical instrument such as this one incorporates a characteristically broad variety of materials. The wood, ivory, cloth, metal, coatings, and textile fiber components each have special preservation needs.

passed down from ancestors. In some cases, antique instruments are still playable, but others must be appreciated just for their beauty or their cultural significance.

Antique musical instruments are not especially fragile as heirlooms go, but unfortunately they can be harmed if they are used for their original purpose: making music. You face the choice of preserving a musical instrument as an antique or attempting to preserve or restore it as a working music maker. The replacement of parts usually needed to make an old instrument play again and keep playing invariably compromises its value as an authentic antique. Moreover, playing places cumulative stresses on old stringed or percussion instruments and causes wear on keyboard and other mechanical instruments. And moisture from the breath tends to cause distortion and cracking in woodwinds and corrosion in brasswinds. Reconditioning, standard maintenance procedures for instruments in use, repairs, and playing all contribute to the deterioration of heirloom musical instruments.

A family piano kept in playing condition will enable present and future generations to learn at the same instrument.

Old instruments reconditioned to play again typically produce neither the sound they did when they were younger nor tones in the range modern ears are accustomed to expect. Paradoxically, if you want to hear what an old instrument sounded like, you may do better to listen to a modern replica built to reproduce the original sound. Playing old instruments may also give you old problems. For example, wood-framed, pre-1840 pianos required much more tuning, even when new, than modern pianos, and they still do if they are to be playable.

Taking Care of Old Musical Instruments

Tension on the strings of such instruments as banjos, violins, and guitars should be kept at a minimum, just enough to keep the soundpost in place in the case of members of the violin family. Changing the tension on older instruments is risky. It should not be done abruptly, and not at all if the structure is weak or the strings are old.

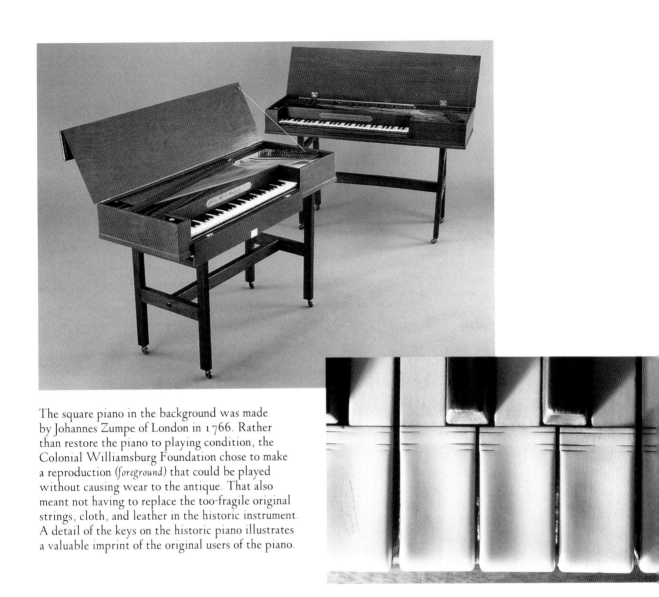

The square piano in the background was made by Johannes Zumpe of London in 1766. Rather than restore the piano to playing condition, the Colonial Williamsburg Foundation chose to make a reproduction (*foreground*) that could be played without causing wear to the antique. That also meant not having to replace the too-fragile original strings, cloth, and leather in the historic instrument. A detail of the keys on the historic piano illustrates a valuable imprint of the original users of the piano.

Pianos and other keyboard instruments such as harpsichords require similar care. A modern grand piano is said to have string tension of about twenty tons on its frame, roughly the weight of an empty boxcar. Old piano wires generally have less tension. They are likely to have more delicate frames. Be especially careful about having an old piano tuned. If the tuner attempts to raise the pitch of a pre-1840 piano to modern expectations, something is very likely to be damaged. Most people who tune pianos today are unfamiliar with standards and methods appropriate to pianos built in the early nineteenth century, making the potential for disaster very great indeed.

Collectors and experts in musical instruments say there is no shame in keeping a nonfunctioning piano in your home. In fact, it is laudable to protect artifacts for their beauty or historic value. Whether a piano is playable or not, it is wise to keep its lid closed to protect the interior from dust. Before you raise the lid of an old piano, be sure pins are intact and working. Modern pianos always should be moved on a dolly, with at least three, and in some cases four, people to do the lifting and moving—not counting you, the supervisor. Very lightweight, pre-1850 pianos are an exception to this rule. Having two strong but gentle movers carry the piano is preferable to using a dolly. If an older piano is too heavy to lift, check to make certain the casters are rolling properly before using them to push the piano. Very old casters rarely function properly.

To protect a brasswind instrument such as a trumpet or a French horn, keep the relative humidity low and avoid skin contact with the brass. If the instrument is played, clear the moisture afterward. It is a good idea to wear clean cotton gloves when handling the piece. Avoid polishing, since most metal polishes will damage the brass. In the antiques market, the natural patina of age is actually preferable to a shiny finish. It is okay to lubricate the valves with the oil or grease normally used by musicians for that instrument.

Woodwinds such as flutes or clarinets are particularly fragile instruments and especially susceptible to damage from moisture introduced when the instrument is played. The player's breath dampens the inner part of the instrument very rapidly, causing it to swell while the outer part remains dry and does not swell. The resulting stress often causes a crack. Woodwind heirlooms are very likely to be dried out. Often the bore has shrunk or become distorted, which makes playing unsatisfactory.

If the instrument must be played, first it should be warmed gradually to body temperature, then "played in" gradually—for only a few seconds at first, allow a day to pass, then play for a minute, allow another day, and so on. It should be swabbed out immediately after it is played. The bore should be recoated periodically with mineral oil or wax, carefully applied so as not to stain

The patina and dents on this horn lend it historic character, evoking images of the schoolboy who first learned to play it.

the surface of the instrument. There are many moisture-proofing "tricks of the trade," such as applying furniture polish or epoxy to the bore. In the long run these methods are harmful to the instrument; they are irreversible and will interfere with later treatments. To safeguard the surface of instruments made of brass, review the chapter on the care of silver and other metals (page 96).

For general care, wooden instruments may be treated like furniture (see page 79). They may be dusted with a clean brush, but you should not oil or polish them, even with preparations that purport to be specifically for instruments. Keep the relative humidity near 50 percent in rooms where instruments are displayed or stored. It is generally a good idea to keep wooden instruments in their cases, but be careful of mold if relative humidity is higher. Make sure there is some ventilation.

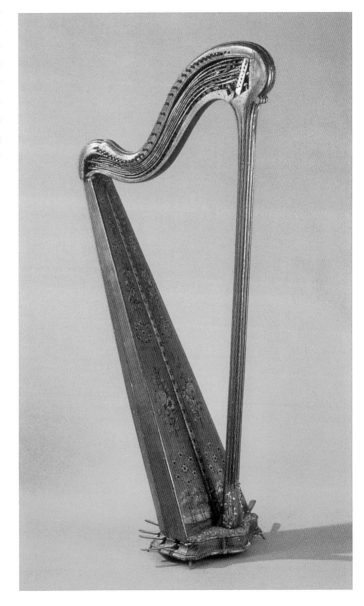

The tension of strings distorts the curved top section of harps just as it distorts most types of historic stringed instruments. For this reason, this harp from c. 1793 is displayed without any strings.

Made in France between 1790 and 1810, this *serinet*, or bird organ, was originally intended to teach birds how to sing. The instrument has been stabilized by conservators rather than restored to playing condition. Sometimes unaltered instruments are more useful as artifacts that enable us to learn how such instruments were made.

Caring for Your Musical Instruments: A Checklist

✓ Avoid placing high tension on stringed (including keyboard) instruments

✓ Avoid sudden increases or decreases in string tension

✓ Move pianos only on dollies and when you have enough people to do the job comfortably

✓ Preserve the natural patina on brass instruments; don't handle them with bare hands or polish them

✓ Keep instruments in rooms with relative humidity at about 50 percent

✓ If you play wooden-bore wind instruments, warm them up and play them in gradually

✓ Clear the moisture from wind instruments immediately after they are played

✓ Do not oil or polish the surfaces of a wooden instrument

Treasures of Nature

The bee is enclosed, and shines preserved in amber, so that it seems enshrined in its own nectar.

—Marcus Valerius Martialis, *Epigrams*

For all of recorded history, travelers have been bringing home from afar objects of beauty, scientific interest, or simple curiosity. Many of these curios are organic at base—shells, horns, teeth, antlers, hair, feathers, skins, wooden masks, basketry, animals, and even mummies. Some of the objects remain as they are found and others are stuffed, carved, painted, or otherwise decorated. Many of these things are treasures in the fullest sense of the term for families lucky enough to inherit them. In a museum, such items might be classified as natural-history specimens, archaeological artifacts, or as ethnographic objects if they are associated with the customs and ceremonies of other cultures. For a family, each is a memento from the life of an interesting ancestor and a reminder of an episode in family lore.

Acquiring, handling, and, if necessary, disposing of many of the pieces discussed in this chapter raise issues that are unique or at least uniquely important

The collection of Native American objects on display in this historical-room exhibit offers a sampling of "treasures of nature." Ethnographic objects such as basketry, masks, leather trunks, and gourd vessels are interesting to keep and display, yet they present a variety of preservation challenges as their organic components are especially fragile.

The cultural integrity of ceremonial objects, such as this African mask, may be diminished if it is cleaned or polished.

for such artifacts. For example, new laws, and increasing enforcement of old laws and international conventions that protect archaeological sites, have dramatically reduced the flow of historic artifacts from their countries of origin. Although there is still a brisk trade in smuggled artifacts, sensitivity to cultural issues—not to mention the risk of apprehension and punishment or confiscation—has increased. The same can be said of illegal specimens of endangered species. Attitudes toward the acquisition and display of Native American cultural artifacts are also changing, as are the laws. In a few cases, ownership of some treasures that have been in a family for many years may be less clear today than a decade ago.

We have also grown more attuned to the importance of the context of many cultural objects. The mud on a ceremonial mask, for example, may be part of the history of its use for religious or cultural purposes. The mask may be of far greater value with that mud—and its cultural integrity—intact than as a cleaned and polished art object. It is useful and fun to learn more about your treasures through research at a local library or a visit to the nearest natural-history museum.

Health and safety of handling are other issues for some important treasures, scientific specimens, and hunting trophies. Some animal specimens have been treated with chemical preservatives or insecticides that we now regard as dangerously toxic.

There are remarkable variations in the physical properties of objects that originated as living things. Sharkskin—*shagreen*—is water repellant and otherwise tough and durable. A feathered headdress is quite fragile. The range of organic materials and the variations in the processes by which they have been treated are vast.

Ivory is a dense dental matter filled with tiny oil channels. Though warm and beautiful, it inevitably yellows and grows brittle as the oil in these channels dries and discolors. Bone is composed of concentrated mineral deposits and is much harder than ivory, on its outer surface at least. Antler combines some of the properties of both. It contains some oil, like ivory, but is much harder, more like

Organic materials can become desiccated and brittle over time. Even slight handling can result in damage.

bone. The horn of a rhinoceros is composed of a hardened conglomerate of hair, while the horns of most other animals are built-up layers of a material something like human fingernails.

Animal furs, feathers, hides, and human hair are protein, prone to drying out and becoming brittle over time. Grasses and reeds used for weaving baskets and mats are composed primarily of cellulose, which is very susceptible to drying, crumbling, and infestation by insect pests.

Hazards

Environmental hazards threaten most things organic. The greatest threats to the treasures families might have are sunlight, significant changes in relative humidity, and insect or rodent infestations. Bright sunlight causes powdering, yellowing, or cracking in various kinds of objects. The attractiveness of even hard materials such as ivory and horn is shortened by heavy doses of sunlight. Low relative humidity leads to drying, powdering, and splitting. High relative humidity causes warping and encourages mold and insect attack. Stuffed animals and birds, furs, leather, feathers, woven grasses and reeds, and even wooden objects such as ceremonial masks are particularly susceptible to attack by insects

Organic objects such as basketry are especially sensitive to high relative humidity and easily susceptible to mold. Mold will quickly flourish given the right conditions.

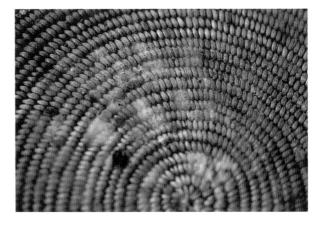

and rodents. Pollutants in the air, particularly sulfur, are harmful as well. Atmospheric sulfur in sufficient quantity is especially damaging to leather, weakening it and making it soft and powdery.

Preserving Your Organic Treasures

Organic treasures should be kept out of direct sunlight and in a controlled climate with the temperature about 72 degrees Fahrenheit and relative humidity around 50 percent. That means they should be kept out of attics and basements, and away from fireplaces, radiators, and other heat sources. Organic objects that are subject to insect or animal infestations can no longer be treated with pesticides or other chemicals, so they should be checked frequently for the first signs of trouble. Since the larvae are what cause damage, it is necessary to look carefully with a bright light into cracks for the evidence of insects (see the discussion of pest control on pages 17–8 for more details).

Because taxidermists formerly used mercuric soap or arsenic in mounting specimens, be especially careful in handling older stuffed birds or animals. Many older specimens were also treated with DDT before it was proscribed. There is no simple way to tell if your object has been treated with these dangerous chemicals. It's a good idea to wear gloves when working with such specimens and not to put your hands on your face. Be sure to wash your hands after handling objects that may have been thus treated.

Old trophy heads require special care in handling since they may have been treated with poisonous substances such as mercury and arsenic. They are also particularly susceptible to insect infestation. Their customary display above the fireplace offers a less than ideal environment for their long-term well being.

Part of the joy of ownership of any treasure comes from showing it off, at least occasionally. You may want to display your treasures in your home or even loan them to a local museum or school for a special exhibition from time to time. A soft or fragile object on display should be secured with interior and exterior supports to help it retain its shape. It should not be tacked or nailed to the wall or hung by its handles or straps. Such an object should be carried by lifting it from below its center of gravity, never by its edges, straps, or handles. If the object is small or has dangling parts, like an Indian headdress, for example, it should be carried on a tray.

Store organic objects in acid-free boxes, using acid-free paper or polyethylene foam as both packing material and filler to help the object retain its shape. Do not use newspaper, or even clean newsprint or other highly acidic material such as wood shavings. Be sure the storage area is climate controlled with steady, moderate relative humidity (50 percent) and visit it at least twice a year to check for insect infestations. If you find an infestation, deal with it promptly.

Treasures of nature need not be exotic. Any object made from organic materials is especially sensitive to environmental conditions of light, temperature, and relative humidity. The historic and economic value of antiques is enhanced when broken or replaced elements are kept with the object.

Cleaning and Repair

Organic objects should be kept clean, but in the least intrusive ways possible. That means that soft objects such as baskets and furs should be vacuumed on low suction with the circular brush attachment covered with a clean piece of cheesecloth. Harder objects such

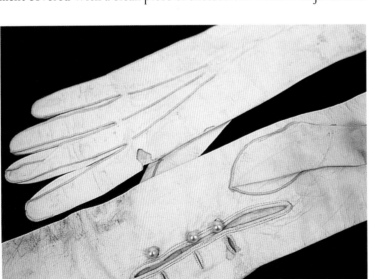

Leather is an organic material found in clothing accessories, books, and furniture. Contrary to popular opinion, leather should never be "dressed," as this actually causes it to deteriorate faster over the long run. Instead, protect leather objects from light, heat, and humidity. These gloves have been damaged by rodents and mildew.

as scrimshaw or antler can be brushed gently with a clean, soft brush. Water or other cleaning agents should never be applied to soft organic pieces.

You should never apply waxes, oils, leather dressings, or other coatings to any object made of organic materials. The use of oils to protect leather has been discontinued for the most part, as the result of careful research on the effects of many leather treatments. Most treatments deteriorate faster than the leather they are supposed to protect.

Caring for Your Natural Treasures: A Checklist

✓ Keep organic objects out of direct sunlight and in stable, moderate relative humidity

✓ Inspect frequently for evidence of insect infestations; never apply insecticides

✓ Secure objects on display with interior and exterior supports; never nail or tack objects to a wall or hang them by their straps or handles

✓ Lift organic material from below the center of gravity, never by straps, edges, or handles

✓ Use acid-free boxes and acid-free paper or polyethylene foam for packing and storing

✓ Don't use newspapers, newsprint, wood, or other acidic materials as packing materials

✓ If the objects are not too dry or fragile, vacuum baskets, fur, mats, and wooden objects on low suction with the brush attachment wrapped with a piece of cheesecloth

✓ Never apply water or cleaning agents

✓ Never apply waxes, oils, leather dressings, or other coatings to any object made of organic materials

Military Mementos

Many families have weapons or other memorabilia passed down from a relative who served in the military. These include souvenir firearms, ceremonial swords, knives, medals, uniforms, and other such mementos. Whether stored or displayed, these objects are often concrete tokens of landmark events in family history—for those who served overseas and for those whose lives were altered in many ways.

Rifles or muskets are composite objects, made of various materials—"lock, stock, and barrel"—and therefore offer special challenges for conservation. Most weapons, including firearms, are made at least partly of metal—steel, iron, bronze, or brass. Most guns also have stocks or handle grips made of wood or some other organic material, and the hilts or hand grips of swords are made of a variety of substances. Uniforms are primarily textiles and leather. Medals or decorations are presented in recognition of service, conduct, or courage. They usually include a metal part, generally a shiny metal such as silver or brass, and a cloth ribbon.

The diversity of components of military memorabilia makes their preservation more complex than if they were made of a single material such as silver or glass. This chapter will cover some highlights of their care. Consult the appropriate chapters in this book for advice on specific materials such as fabrics, brass, or leather.

Relics of military service are a source of family pride. The fabric ribbon on this commemorative medal is inherently more fragile than the metal and so will deteriorate faster.

Because most are composite objects, antique firearms are at special risk from high, low, and widely fluctuating relative humidity. Fluctuations may cause wooden stocks or the various organic materials in pistol handles to swell or shrink rapidly and to split or break loose from the metal parts to which they are attached. Chemicals in the air, as well as the normal oils and salts on human skin, pose another threat if they come in contact with the metal parts of medals and weapons. Corrosion caused by these chemicals mars the appearance of beautifully finished medals, knives, swords, or firearms. Long or repeated exposure will cause serious pitting. High temperatures and, even worse, the ultraviolet rays in direct sunlight accelerate many of the chemical processes that promote deterioration and cause organic materials such as gun stocks to fade. Last, improper cleaning and storage may be the greatest culprits in the destruction of treasured weapons.

Guns are composite objects in which various elements have different needs and can interact. Acids emitted by the wood used for the handle can corrode the metal. Gunpowder residue is also a common cause of corrosion in historic guns.

Caring for Your Heirloom Weapons and Military Souvenirs

The ideal way to take care of your military treasures is by minimizing their exposure to these hazards. That means keeping them in a room with a steady temperature of about 70 degrees Fahrenheit and relative humidity around 50 percent. This rules out most basements and attics, as well as places near heating vents or fireplaces. If you can, keep your sword or firearm in a glass case to reduce exposure to dust and pollution in the air. Protect it from sunlight, perhaps by using treated glass or ultraviolet film on windows. Place *scavengers*, or pollutant-absorbent materials such as activated charcoal, in the display cases, replacing them as they lose effectiveness. When you store or display any object, make sure it is not in contact with acidic wood, wool fabric, or acidic paper. Do not use adhesives of any kind to mount your treasures for display. Polyester or polyethylene foam cutouts may be used to hold the weapon in place for display.

A medal can be displayed in its presentation case if the case is lined with acid-free tissue to keep the medal from contact with any material that might contain acid or release harmful gases in the process of deterioration. Although presentation cases are not ideal if they are made of wood or contain organic linings, they at least provide physical support and exclude damaging sunlight.

You should wear clean cotton gloves when handling the metal parts of memorabilia to make sure you do not leave fingerprints. They can quickly be etched permanently into the blade of a beautiful presentation sword, for example. Weapons and medals should be dusted frequently with a magnetic cloth or a clean, soft brush, since dust is a great collector of moisture and pollutants. The ribbons attached to medals may be vacuumed on gentle suction with cheesecloth secured over the nozzle of the brush attachment, so that any loose small pieces (or in this case, perhaps the

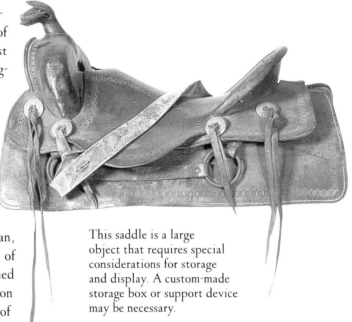

This saddle is a large object that requires special considerations for storage and display. A custom-made storage box or support device may be necessary.

Above: A storage box was constructed especially for this medal using archival quality materials. The polyethylene foam provides support, the box protection, and the fabric padding.

Right: Previous storage of the medal in a candle box was less than ideal for a variety of reasons. For one, the discoloration of the tissue paper is a clear indication that it is acidic and will cause pitting or corrosion of the metal over time. The original presentation case would have been a better choice.

whole ribbon and medal) will not be drawn into the vacuum. Ribbons that are already split or tattered should not be vacuumed.

The instinct to keep medals and weapons looking as shiny as possible is natural. Because polishes contain abrasives, however, some of the metal is lost with each polishing. Polishing can be particularly damaging if the piece is plated or contains fine detail work. The historic, aesthetic, and monetary value of your piece is at least slightly reduced with each polishing, and it may be substantially reduced by frequent polishing with highly abrasive compounds. If it is necessary to clean iron or steel treasures, use only denatured alcohol or mineral spirits applied with a cotton swab or a soft rag, never commercial cleaners or polishes. Read the warnings and follow safety directions carefully since these solutions can be toxic as well as flammable. (See page 96 for more on the care of the silver and copper alloy parts of medals.) If you keep a firearm stored in a safe place, protected from dust and with a steady, moderate relative humidity, you won't need to oil it. It is better not to do so, since oil will slowly congeal and cause corrosion.

Keep medals and weapons such as this sword dust free, since accumulated dust will collect moisture and pollutants. The temptation to polish is great, but it should be kept to a minimum, if done at all.

Firearms were designed to be lethal, and age alone does nothing to make them less so. Exercise all the care in handling old firearms that you would use in handling new weapons. Be aware of federal, state, and local laws governing guns and ammunition, particular those governing gun safety. Historic firearms should never be loaded or fired. Bullets or charges may become lodged in old weapons when they are loaded after a long period of disuse. The risk of harm from firing is high because modern powders exceed the capacities of old weapons, and because an old weapon may have hidden cracks or damage that could make it explode in your hands. Powder residues are highly corrosive, and cleaning the inside of the barrel, which is necessary after firing, is itself problematic since it requires the use of solvents that may trickle into the firing mechanism of the gun and cause corrosion during prolonged storage.

Part of preserving history is recording and documenting
information. It is wonderful when ancestors have
recorded the names of the individuals in a group photograph. This information is best recorded on a separate
sheet of paper that is coded to the photograph.

Caring for Military Mementos: A Checklist

✓ Keep historic metal objects and weapons in a room with
moderate temperature and steady relative humidity of
about 50 percent

✓ Keep your military treasures out of direct sunlight and
contact with wood or other acidic materials

✓ Wear clean cotton gloves when handling medals and
metal parts of weapons

✓ Dust your treasures with a clean brush or magnetic cloth

✓ Don't use commercial cleaners or polishes on metal parts

✓ Don't load or fire historic firearms

Little Friends:
Dolls, Teddy Bears, and Toy Soldiers

"I have been Foolish and Deluded," said he, "and I am a Bear of No Brain at All."

*"You're the Best Bear in All the World,"
said Christopher Robin soothingly.*

—A.A. Milne, *Winnie the Pooh*

Nothing can put us in touch with the past as quickly as a toy. Our first teddy bear, now propped on a closet shelf, or the set of lead soldiers a favorite uncle delighted in showing us, elicit fond memories. Antique dolls, from a homemade rag doll to an elegant china princess, illuminate for us the childhood of parents or grandparents. With sensible care and a little extra effort, these personal treasures can be preserved and passed along to a new generation.

Dolls

Dolls have been made from various materials: wood, glazed porcelain, bisque, papier-mâché, *composition* (usually a mix of sawdust and glue), wax, metal, plastic, and fabric. Many have heads and bodies composed of different substances. Thus, it is important to know which element of the doll is the most delicate and then follow the appropriate guidelines for that particular material. Say, for example, you have a nineteenth-century doll that you want to display. Indirect sunlight and wooden shelving may be no threat to the doll's porcelain head, but the dainty fabric of her dress should be protected. Therefore, you would treat the doll as you would an antique costume: limit the exposure to light, and keep the doll on glass or metal shelves in a stable environment. If a doll has a head shaped from wax, on the other hand, shielding it from heat and too much handling would be the top priorities.

Rag dolls have been around for centuries, although there are few surviving examples more than one hundred fifty years old. They range in style from primitive bundles of rags and string to lovely cloth dolls from famous toy manufacturers. They wear a wide variety of textiles and, depending on when they were made, may be stuffed with anything from sand and sawdust to polyester. Their features are painted or sewn on, and they may sport delicate ornaments and even wigs made of human hair. Because of their make up, rag dolls are very fragile. Follow the guidelines for teddy bears in caring for them. Refer to the chapters in this book on fabrics, ceramics, and organic treasures to help you preserve other types of heirloom dolls.

As the baby-boom generation ages, mass-produced, plastic dolls like Barbie™ are becoming valued for sentimental reasons and prized as collectibles. Often more than one kind of plastic has been used to make the same doll. Plastics are not as tough as we often assume. All plastics can be damaged by light, heat, pollution, and very high or very low relative humidity. Certain plastics, such as celluloid (cellulose nitrate) and polyvinyl chloride (PVC), give off fumes that are destructive to the objects containing them and to other materials. Flexible PVC has been the primary material used in making many toys and most dolls beginning in the late 1940s; celluloid was used even earlier.

Display and store plastic dolls in a cool, dry, dim environment; never expose them to direct sunlight, which will cause discoloration and fading. Make sure that dolls made of polyvinyl chloride and other early plastics are stored in well-ventilated boxes. Cover them lightly with acid-free tissue to protect them from dust. An odor resembling vinegar or camphor, or a surface that is sticky, powdery, darkened, or cracked, are all signs of deterioration and the possible emission of

Twentieth-century dolls are increasingly becoming collector's items. The plastics used in their manufacture have unique qualities affecting their preservation.

harmful gases. Any doll with these symptoms should be separated from other heirlooms.

If a doll needs cleaning, try first to remove the dirt with a soft, dry brush. If necessary, use a cotton swab lightly dampened with water. Dab with clean water on a cotton swab to rinse, and then pat dry with a cotton cloth. Do not use solvents because these can mar and even dissolve some plastics. Doll hair can present complicated problems. Synthetic hair should be combed very gently so as not to pull fibers.

Original clothes on heirloom dolls should be preserved whenever possible, even if the articles are very worn. Follow the guidelines for fabric care on page 73 and make padding from acid-free tissue paper to help keep the shape of the hair and clothing on dolls in storage. Many dolls are best stored face down to prevent distortion of hair or hats, and to prevent the separation of movable eyes from their mounting brackets inside the doll's head.

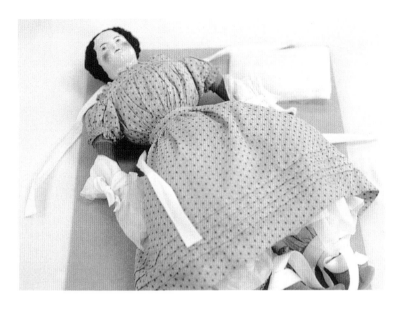

This doll has been prepared for storage. Tissue has been stuffed into her dress to help preserve it and avoid creases.

Dolls of any age can be very valuable and seriously harmed by careless treatment and inexpert repairs. Many books on collecting and restoring dolls are available, but they often recommend risky measures. Leave the repair and conservation of valuable dolls to professionals. If you are fortunate enough to inherent or acquire an antique dollhouse, don't attempt to restore it yourself or let chil-

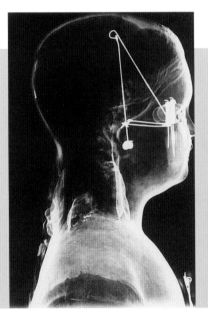

The fabric of this doll's dress deteriorates at a much faster rate than its papier-mâché head, hands, and feet. Further, the mechanisms within dolls that cause their eyes to move may become dysfunctional. Storing a doll face down will prevent separation of the eyes from their mounting brackets.

Not only the dolls, but also their accessories, such as this charming wooden dollhouse, are fun to care for and pass down through generations.

dren play with it unsupervised. Based on the materials in its construction, consult this and other chapters for general care guidelines.

Teddy Bears and Other Stuffed Toys

Children have been playing with plush bears and other stuffed toys since the late nineteenth century, but it was not until president Theodore Roosevelt adopted a bear as his mascot that "teddy bears" soared in popularity with children and collectors. Originally they were constructed from mohair, often with wood-wool, cork, or horsehair stuffing. During World War II, some were made from sheepskin. Artificial silk-plush was first used in the 1920s, and foam rubber and polyester stuffing introduced in the 1950s. Limbs were attached with card disks and metal pins and, later, plastic joints.

Teddy bears are inherently delicate creatures, subject to damage by dust, extremes of temperature and relative humidity, direct sunlight, frequent (even loving) handling, and pests such as carpet beetles and moths. Leave repairs of treasured bears to experts. Lightly

Treasured childhood friends, such as this Raggedy Ann doll, carry the wear and tear of a child's love. (At far left is the same doll, seen in a 1949 home movie.) Evidence of such affection adds to the historical interest and sentimental value.

A collection of toy soldiers handsomely displayed and safely kept on glass shelving.

dust bears with a soft bristle brush or use a vacuum cleaner operating on the lowest setting with the brush attachment covered with cheesecloth. Never use water on old bears; this can result in rusted metal parts, stained fabrics, and mold. Inspect them regularly for signs of pests, consulting with a specialist if you detect a problem before undertaking any treatment on your own.

Display teddy bears in cabinets out of direct sunlight and away from sources of heat. Store them wrapped in acid-free tissue in an acid-free box. Use the tissue to pad any costume the bear might be wearing. Do not use plastic bags or store teddy bears with aromatic substances such as mothballs or cedar shavings.

GAMES

Many families have games that have stayed in the family for more than a generation. It goes without saying that games are more fun, and more valuable, if all of the pieces are kept together—especially if the game is in the original box and the box is in good condition.

Toy Soldiers

Most sets of collectible toy soldiers are made from lead. Often, by the time you have inherited or acquired them, many years of play have worn away paint and bent or broken off the projecting parts of limbs and weapons. Attempting to straighten bent swords is likely to result in more breakage, and repainting soldiers will reduce their value as antiques. Like other objects made from lead and lead alloys, toy soldiers are particularly susceptible to damage from the acidic gases in wood and cardboard. Display them on glass rather than wooden shelves. Store lead soldiers in acid-free boxes and keep them in an environment of low relative humidity; dampness will accelerate corrosion. For care of more modern toy soldiers and "action figures," follow the advice for care, display, and storage of plastic dolls.

Little Friends: A Checklist

✓ Dolls may be composed of a variety of substances; follow care guidelines for the most delicate materials

✓ Keep plastic dolls in a cool, dim, dry, and well-ventilated environment; isolate dolls or other plastic toys that are beginning to deteriorate

✓ Dust dolls regularly with a soft brush; if it is necessary to clean plastic dolls, use only water

✓ Leave the repair and conservation of antique dolls and dollhouses to experts

✓ Protect teddy bears, rag dolls, and other stuffed toys from sunlight, heat, extremes in relative humidity, and pests

✓ Keep lead toy soldiers in a dry environment and protect them from the acid in wood and cardboard

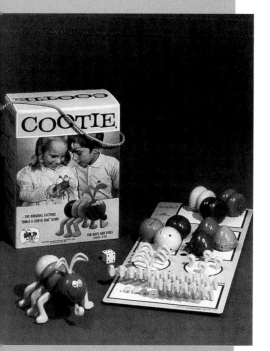

Because they are rare, toys in their original packaging have great value as collector's items.

Security and Insurance

Because your family treasures are precious to you, be sure to protect them through security measures and insurance coverage. Items in your collection can be defaced, broken, stolen, damaged by water, or destroyed by fire. Disaster, both natural and manmade, can strike when you least expect it. Take measures to reduce the risk of damage and destruction to your collection as you do with your home and bank accounts. These measures can be as overt as the installation of a security system, smoke detectors, a sump pump, in some cases even a fire-suppression system. Security measures can also be subtle, such as good housekeeping practices and regular inspections to monitor changing conditions that may present new risks.

The goal is keeping your heirlooms free from danger. Know the ever-present risks and take steps to reduce them. Your home is an envelope that holds and protects your possessions: damage to that envelope will result in damage to the contents within. Diligent home maintenance of roofs and windows, even pruning of tree limbs, is one way to protect your treasures. Create a fire-safe environment by controlling the amount and location of flammable materials and their proximity to heat and energy sources. Remember that damage is not always dramatic. An unnoticed or ignored leak around the tub upstairs can insidiously damage objects hanging on the wall downstairs.

Proper insurance can soften the blow should disaster strike. For most of us, the objects within our homes are protected through our homeowner's insurance policy. Make sure you know what your policy covers and that it is adequate. Especially valuable items may warrant special coverage through riders on your homeowner's policy or, in some cases, special fine-art policies. An appraisal documenting a professional description of an object together with an estimate of its worth is helpful in determining adequate coverage.

It is common to protect large financial investments such as homes and bank accounts with insurance and security procedures. Consider the emotional investment you have in your family treasures. Though your collection may not have a large monetary value, it is irreplaceable and so deserves these protective measures, too.

Ten Tips for the Care of Flood-Damaged Family Heirlooms and Other Valuables

In event of a disaster, your first response is crucial. Heritage Preservation and the American Institute for Conservation of Historic and Artistic Works (AIC) offer the following general recommendations for homeowners who have had family heirlooms and other valuables damaged by flooding:

1. If the object is still wet, rinse with clear water or a fine hose spray. Clean off dry silt and debris from your belongings with soft brushes or dab with damp cloths. Try not to grind debris into objects; overly energetic cleaning will cause scratching. Dry with a clean, soft cloth. Use plastic or rubber gloves for your own protection.

2. Air dry objects indoors if possible. Sunlight and heat may dry certain materials too quickly, causing splits, warping, and buckling. If possible, remove contents from wet objects and furniture prior to drying. Storing damp items in sealed plastic bags will cause mold to develop. If objects are to be transported in plastic bags, keep bags open and air circulating within.

MONITOR AND BE VIGILANT

✓ Regularly inspect areas where your treasures are displayed
and stored for potential threats such as leaking pipes, broken
windows, malfunctioning locks, overloaded electrical
equipment, or flammable materials

✓ Make sure smoke detectors and other warning devices are
operating properly

✓ Check and maintain fire extinguishers to be certain they will
operate properly when needed

TAKE EXTRA PRECAUTIONS FOR PARTICULARLY VALUABLE OR PRECIOUS ITEMS

✓ Consider storing in a fire-resistant safe or safe-deposit box

✓ The ever-present threat of theft may warrant installation of
a security system

✓ Insure items that are particularly valuable

✓ Maintain a list of items, complete with photographs and
appraisals if you have them, in a secure location off-premises,
such as a safe-deposit box or relative's home

BE PREPARED THAT DISASTER MIGHT STRIKE

✓ Consider location of water and fuel pipes when planning storage

✓ Take special precautions to minimize potential damage.
For instance, raising storage boxes off the floor by placing them
on shelves or plastic pallets may keep them dry in the event of
a flood. Cover boxes and objects in polyethylene plastic to
mitigate water damage. Store flammable household products
separately— if space is limited, consider storing in fireproof
metal cabinets. Temporarily relocate precious objects during
construction and major cleaning projects

✓ Familiarize yourself with basic disaster response procedures,
for instance, be sure you know how to cut off the water supply
in the event of a burst pipe

✓ Have disaster mitigation tools such as fire extinguishers on hand

3. The best way to inhibit the growth of mold and mildew is to reduce humidity. Increase air flow with fans, open windows, air conditioners, and dehumidifiers. Moderate light exposure (open shades, leave basement lights on) can also reduce mold and mildew.

4. Remove heavy deposits of mold growth from walls, baseboards, floors, and other household surfaces with commercially available disinfectants. Avoid the use of disinfectants on historic wallpapers. Follow manufacturers' instructions but avoid splattering or contact with objects and wallpapers, as disinfectants may damage objects. Note: Exposure to molds can have serious health consequences such as respiratory problems, skin and eye irritation, and infections. The use of protective gear, including a respirator with a particulate filter, disposable plastic gloves, goggles or protective eyewear, and coveralls or a lab coat, is therefore essential.

5. If objects are broken or begin to fall apart, place all broken pieces, bits of veneer, and detached parts in clearly labeled, open containers. Do not attempt to repair objects until completely dry or, in the case of important materials, until you have consulted with a professional conservator.

6. Documents, books, photographs, and works of art on paper may be extremely fragile when wet; use caution when handling. Free the edges of prints and paper objects in mats and frames, if possible. These should be allowed to air dry. Rinse mud off wet photographs with clear water, but do not touch surfaces. Sodden books and papers should also be air dried or kept in a refrigerator or freezer until they can be treated by a professional conservator.

7. Textiles, leather, and other "organic" materials will also be affected severely by exposure to water and should be allowed to air dry. Shaped objects, such as garments or baskets, should be supported by gently padding with toweling or uninked, uncoated paper. Renew padding when it becomes saturated with water. Dry clean or launder textiles and carpets as you normally would.

8. Remove wet paintings from the frame but not the stretcher. Air dry, face up, away from direct sunlight. Make sure there is airflow to the underside.

9. Furniture finishes and painting surfaces may develop a white haze or bloom from contact with water and humidity. These problems do not require immediate attention; consult a professional conservator for treatment.

10. Rinse metal objects exposed to flood waters, mud, or silt with clear water and dry immediately with a clean, soft cloth. Allow heavy mud deposits on large metal objects, such as sculpture, to dry. Caked mud can be removed later. Consult a professional conservator for further treatment.

For more detailed information on salvaging family treasures, visit the Heritage Preservation web site and see the information provided by the National Task Force on Emergency Response (www.heritagepreservation.org/PROGRAMS/taskfer.htm).

This *fraktur* shows adhesive damage. It has since undergone professional conservation treatment.

Finding Professional Help

There will be occasions when you should consider calling upon the help of a professional when caring for your treasures. Choosing the right professional is much like choosing a doctor, so use the same criteria: make sure they are professionally trained and consider whether their specialty matches your needs. Talk to friends who might have used similar services. Ask the specialist for references and be sure to check them. A description of professionals who may assist you and how to find them follows.

A *conservator* is a professional whose primary occupation is the care, restoration and repair of objects, collections, specimens, structures, or sites. Through specialized education, knowledge, training, and experience, a conservator formulates and implements conservation activities, including examination, treatment, preventive care, and documentation. Conservators specialize in object types, some of which are paper, photographs, furniture, architecture, paintings, and decorative arts. To locate a conservator, contact:

The American Institute for Conservation
of Historic and Artistic Works (AIC)
1717 K Street, NW, Suite 200
Washington, DC 20006-5342
202-452-9545
http://aic.stanford.edu

This image is actually a crayon enlargement, a photographic portrait reworked with crayons or chalk to have the appearance of a drawing. Damaged by vandals, this family treasure was feared to be lost forever. Delicate and painstaking professional conservation treatment included removing dirt, mending tears, backing with Japanese paper, inpainting and remounting.

AIC's Guide to Conservation Services is a free referral service that also provides the helpful brochure *Guidelines for Selecting a Conservator*.

An *appraiser* is an expert who is qualified by education, training, and experience to evaluate an object and set a value on it. This evaluation or appraisal is a professional opinion, usually written, of the market value of a property whose price is not easily determined, such as art and historical objects. Rather than being just an "educated guess," the professional appraiser's conclusions are based on prescribed methods of evaluation, research, and report writing. Appraisals are usually required when a property is sold, taxed, insured, or financed. For more information, including how to find an appraiser, contact:

American Society of Appraisers
555 Herndon Parkway, Suite 125
Herndon, VA 20170-5248
703-478-2228
www.apo.com
    You can locate an appraiser by calling 800-ASA-VALU or searching on-line. The ASA accredits appraisers through written examinations, sample appraisal reports, and screening for ethical behavior. Each accredited member of the American Society of Appraisers has earned a professional designation in one or more specialties.

Art Dealers Association of America
575 Madison Avenue
New York, NY 10022-2511
212-940-8590
www.artdealers.org
    Since 1962, the ADAA has appraised works of art for tax purposes through its Appraisal Service.

International Society of Appraisers
Riverview Plaza Office Park
16040 Christensen Road, Suite 102
Seattle, WA 98188-2965
206-241-0359
http://isa-appraisers.org
    Toll-free appraisal referral and information line 888-472-5587.

Their helpful Web site has basic information about appraisals, including "Seven Questions to Ask When Hiring an Appraiser." The ISA certifies and accredits members.

A *professional genealogist* can help you research your family history. Genealogy is a popular pastime and much information and assistance is available for the do-it-yourselfer over the Internet, in books, and through genealogical societies. However, you may also wish to consult with an experienced researcher. Some organizations that can help you locate a professional genealogist or provide research assistance and resources are:

Association of Professional Genealogists
P.O. Box 40393
Denver, CO 80204-0393
www.apgen.org
    Publishes a directory of members with indices to assist in finding researchers. Also offers a brochure, *So You're Going to Hire a Professional Genealogist.*

Federation of Genealogical Societies
P.O. Box 200940
Austin, TX 78720-0940
888-347-1500
www.fgs.org/
    More than five hundred genealogical societies are members of FGS. The FGS/Ancestry's Society Hall can help you locate a society near you.

National Genealogical Society
Glebe House
4527 Seventeenth Street North
Arlington, VA 22207-2399
800-473-0060
www.ngsgenealogy.org/
    The NGS assists members in tracing family histories by providing educational opportunities and resources, including *The Beginner's Kit,* a home-study course titled *American Genealogy: A Basic Course,* and an on-line course titled *Introduction to Genealogy.*

This mounted document has become discolored by its wooden backing. The acids in wood are very harmful to paper.

Finding Materials and Tools for Cleaning, Display, and Storage

A plethora of products are advertised today as "acid-free," "preservation safe," or "museum quality." Beware: such claims can be incorrect and misleading because they are not standardized. So called "acid-free" products may not be acidic at the point of purchase, but they may develop damaging acids as they age. "Preservation safe" on self-adhesive album pages is nonsensical. "Museum quality" can be a meaningless lure, used in the same way as "new and improved" on laundry detergent.

"Archival-quality" is the term used by the conservation profession for materials that resist deterioration themselves, provide physical protection and support, and don't damage their contents chemically. Unfortunately this term is also misused. For quality assurance, purchase supplies from vendors that specialize in conservation and preservation materials.

Selection of materials for the care of your personal treasures is idiosyncratic. Before you shop, make sure you have a clear understanding of the nature of your objects and the prevailing conditions where they will be stored or displayed.

Listed below are some suppliers of preservation materials that will sell in small quantities to individuals. This list is neither exhaustive nor an endorsement. Perusing catalogs from a number of vendors will allow you to compare costs and assess the range of products available.

Archival Products
P.O. Box 1413
Des Moines, IA 50305-1413
800-526-5640
www.archival.com

Archivart
7 Caesar Place
Moonachie, NJ 07074-1702
800-804-8428
www.archivart.com

Conservation Resources International,
    L.L.C.
8000-H Forbes Place
Springfield, VA 22151-2203
800-634-6932
www.conservationresources.com

Forever Yours/Keepsafe Systems
570 King Street West
Toronto, Ontario M5V 1M3
Canada
800-683-4696
www.gowncare.com

Gaylord Bros.
P.O. Box 4901
Syracuse, NY 13221-4901
800-448-6160
www.gaylord.com

Light Impressions
439 Monroe Avenue
P.O. Box 940
Rochester, NY 14603-0940
800-828-6216
www.lightimpressionsdirect.com

Metal Edge, Inc.
6340 Bandini Blvd.
Commerce, CA 90040-3116
800-862-2228
www.metaledgeinc.com

University Products
517 Main Street
P.O. Box 101
Holyoke, MA 01041-5514
800-628-1912
www.universityproducts.com

Books to Help You

These books have sound advice to help you care for your precious objects. The growing popularity of hobbies like scrapbooking and programs such as *The Antiques Roadshow* have prompted numerous books on making family memory books and caring for antiques and collectibles. Some of them purport to use "archival" and "preservation-safe" methods. As a general rule, methods advocated by the conservation profession do not encourage active alteration or destruction of original material, such as cropping historic photographs and removing historic finishes. Be wary of sources that suggest such techniques or harsh cleaning methods. As always, for further guidance, contact a professional conservator.

Bachmann, Konstanze, ed. *Conservation Concerns: A Guide for Collectors and Curators.* Washington, DC: Smithsonian Institution Press, 1992.

Baldwin, Gordon. *Looking at Photographs.* Malibu, CA: J. Paul Getty Museum, 1991.

Bark, Jared. "Preservation/Conservation Framing." *Picture Framing Magazine* supplement. Manalapan, NJ: Picture Framing Magazine, 1993.

Clapp, Anne F. *Curatorial Care of Works of Art on Paper.* New York: Nick Lyons Books, 1987.

Davis, Nancy. *Handle With Care: Preserving Your Heirlooms.* Rochester, NY: Rochester Museum and Science Center, 1991.

Eaton, George. *Conservation of Photographs*, Kodak Publication No. F-40. Rochester, NY: Eastman Kodak Company, 1985.

Ellis, Margaret H. *The Care of Prints and Drawings.* Thousand Oaks, CA: Altamira Press, 1987.

Fortson, Judith. *Disaster Planning and Recovery: A How-To-Do-It Manual for Librarians and Archivists.* New York: Neal-Schuman Publishers, Inc., 1992.

Greenfield, Jane. *The Care of Fine Books.* New York, NY: Nick Lyons Books [Distributed by Lyons and Burford], 1988.

Heritage Preservation, ed. *Caring for Your Collections: Preserving and Protecting Your Art and Other Collectibles.* New York: Harry N. Abrams, Inc. 1992.

Heritage Preservation and National Park Service. *Caring for Your Historic House*. New York: Harry N. Abrams, Inc. 1998.

MacLeish, A. Bruce. *The Care of Antiques and Historical Collections*. 2d ed. Thousand Oaks, CA: Altamira Press, 1985.

Mailand, Harold F. *Considerations for the Care of Textiles and Costumes: A Handbook for the Non-Specialist*. Indianapolis, IN: Indianapolis Museum of Art, 1980.

Martin, Elizabeth. *Collecting and Preserving Old Photographs*. London: William Collins Sons & Co., Ltd., 1988.

McGiffin, Jr., Robert F. *Furniture Care and Conservation*. 3d ed. Thousand Oaks, CA: Altamira Press, 1992.

Ogden, Sherelyn, ed. *Preservation of Library and Archival Materials: A Manual*, 3d ed. Andover, MA: Northeast Document Conservation Center, 1999.

Perkinson, Roy L., and Francis W. Dolloff. *How to Care for Works of Art on Paper*, 4th ed. Boston, MA: Museum of Fine Arts, 1985.

Reilly, James M. *The Care and Identification of 19th-Century Photographic Prints*. Kodak Publication G-28. Rochester, NY: Eastman Kodak Company, 1986.

Sandwith, Hermione, and Sheila Staunton. *National Trust Manual of Housekeeping*. Middlesex, England: Penguin Books in association with the National Trust, 1985.

Simpson, Mette T., and Michael Huntley. *Sotheby's Caring for Antiques: The Complete Guide to Handling, Cleaning, Display, and Restoration*. Old Tappan, NJ: Simon and Schuster Trade, 1993.

Smith, Merrily A., and Margaret Brown. *Matting & Hinging of Works of Art on Paper*. Washington, DC: Library of Congress, 1981.

Snyder, Jill. *Caring for Your Art: A Guide for Artists, Collectors, Galleries, and Art Institutions*, rev.ed. New York, NY: Allworth Press, 1996.

Stout, George L. *The Care of Pictures*. New York: Dover Publications Inc., 1975.

Trinkley, Michael, and Debi Hacker. *Preserving Your Family Treasures*, 2d ed. Columbia, SC: Chicora Foundation, Inc., 1998.

Williams, Marc A. *Keeping it All Together-The Preservation and Care of Historic Furniture*. 2d ed. Worthington, OH: Ohio Antique Review, 1990.

The poor-quality wood pulp paper used to print this magazine has become brittle and too fragile to touch.

Other Resources To Help You

Many museums, conservation organizations, and conservators in private practice offer reliable, easy-to-understand information at little or no cost. Your favorite or local museum may be able to help you.

Increasingly, information is becoming available online. There are also reliable government resources, including state archives and historical societies, the Library of Congress (http://lcweb.loc.gov/preserv/), and *National Park Service Conserv O Grams* (http://www.cr.nps.gov/csd/).

The American Institute for Conservation of Historic and Artistic Works offers eleven brochures on caring for objects such as home videotape, photographs, textiles and architecture, as well as how to locate and select a conservator. Its Guide to Conservation Services can help you locate a professional conservator in private practice in your area.

American Institute for Conservation of Historic and Artistic Works
1717 K Street, NW, Suite 200
Washington, DC 20006-5342
202-452-9545
http://aic.stanford.edu

Additionally, the Regional Alliance for Preservation can link you to regional conservation centers that may have brochures and conservators to help you.

Regional Alliance for Preservation
c/o Amigos Library Services, Inc.
Imaging and Preservation Services
14400 Midway Road
Dallas, TX 75244-3509
800-843-8482
http://www.rap-arcc.org

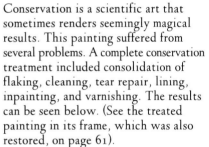

Conservation is a scientific art that sometimes renders seemingly magical results. This painting suffered from several problems. A complete conservation treatment included consolidation of flaking, cleaning, tear repair, lining, inpainting, and varnishing. The results can be seen below. (See the treated painting in its frame, which was also restored, on page 61).

Glossary

ACETATE FILM Called "safety film," this photographic film base was introduced in 1923. Early acetate and diacetate film base are especially prone to shrinkage and embrittlement.

ACID A class of chemicals having a pH less than 7.0. Acids contained in objects or in contact with them generally cause deterioration.

ACID-FREE Term used for materials with pH value of 7.1 or higher.

ACID MIGRATION Transfer of acidity from an acidic material to a less acidic material through physical contact or vapors.

ACIDITY The quality of being acid.

ACRYLIC A plastic noted for transparency, light weight, weather resistance, color fastness and rigidity. Important in preservation because of its resistance to change over time.

ALKALINE A class of chemicals having a pH value of 7.1 or higher. Used to neutralize acids.

AMBROTYPE A positive picture made of a photographic negative on glass backed by a dark surface.

ANODIZED ALUMINUM Aluminum subjected to electrolytic action in order to coat with a protective film.

ARCHIVAL QUALITY Term used to indicate that products, particularly paper products, are chemically stable and, thus, suitable for preservation purposes. There are no official standards of archival quality.

BRITTLE PAPER Paper that crumbles or deteriorates to the touch.

BUFFER A chemical reserve that helps maintain a pH range by counteracting acids or bases. It can be added during manufacture or deacidification.

CALCIUM CARBONATE An alkaline chemical that is used as a buffer in paper and storage boxes to inhibit the formation and migration of acids.

CELLULOSE Chief component of cell walls of all plants and plant products, including paper, wood, and cloth.

CELLULOID Plastic derived from cellulose.

CHEMICAL STABILITY The ability of certain chemical bonds to resist degradation when exposed to other chemicals. Not easily decomposed or otherwise modified chemically. A desirable characteristic for materials used in preservation. Also referred to as inert or stable.

CLAMSHELL BOX A one-piece box with hinged lid.

CONSERVATION The profession devoted to the preservation of cultural property for the future. Conservation activities include examination, documentation, treatment, and preventive care, supported by research and education.

CULTURAL PROPERTY Objects, collections, specimens, structures, or sites identified as having artistic, historic, scientific, religious, or social significance.

DAGUERREOTYPE An early photograph produced on a silver or a silver-covered copper plate.

DEACIDIFICATION A treatment that neutralizes acids and deposits an acid buffer in paper through application of a mild

Another example of profound effects of conservation treatment. This twentieth-century family portrait was yellowed by a natural resin varnish that oxidized. A professional conservation studio cleaned and revarnished it with a stable synthetic acrylic-resin varnish, returning it to the original color scheme.

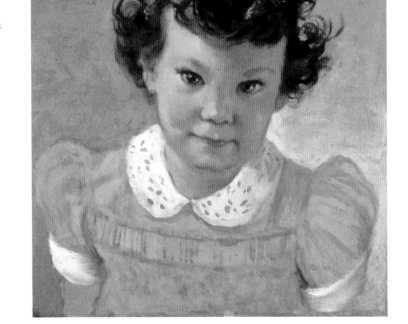

148

alkaline solution. Though the buffer counteracts future acid damage, the process does not reverse prior damage.

DOCUMENTATION The permanent recording of information. Important for both an object's provenance and conservation history.

ENCAPSULATION A protective enclosure for papers and other flat objects made by placing the item between two sheets of polyester film and sealing the edges with double-sided, pH-balanced tape. The enclosure protects the item from pollutants, fungi, and excessive handling. Because the object is not adhered to the polyester, it can be removed easily.

EPHEMERA Term for objects intended to last for a short time, such as ticket stubs, playbills, and pressed corsages.

EXAMINATION Process in which a conservator investigates an object's structure, materials, and condition, including identifying the extent and causes of alteration and deterioration.

FIBER-OPTIC LIGHTS Thin, transparent fibers of glass or plastic that transmit light through their length by internal reflections. Create less heat than other sources.

FLUORESCENT LAMP Produces light using mercury vapor. Has a higher UV output than an incandescent lamp but less than the amount of UV in natural light. Recommend UV filtration.

FOXING Reddish-brown spots on paper caused by an interaction between fungi and iron salts. The fungi will not develop at relative humidity levels below 75 percent.

FRASS Insect excrement. Sometimes mistaken for sawdust, as in the case of wood-boring insects.

GLASSINE A translucent, smooth, thin paper that resists passage of air and dirt.

HALOGEN LAMP Produces light using halogen gas. Has a higher UV output than an incandescent lamp, but less than the amount of UV in natural light. Recommend UV filtration.

HYGROSCOPIC The ability of a material to absorb or release moisture. This property makes objects vulnerable to damage from frequent or dramatic changes in relative humidity.

INCANDESCENT LAMP Produces light by heating a metal filament to luminescence. Has low UV component but gives off damaging heat.

INTERLEAVE To insert blank leaves, or pages, in a book or album in order to separate pages from one another. Acid-free leaves slow the deterioration of materials in scrapbooks. Interleaving with blotter or waxed paper or white paper towels will help dry damp books.

IRON GALL INK A mixture of iron sulfate, oak galls, arabic gum, and water used from the seventeenth to early twentieth century. This ink fades and eventually burns through paper due to its acidity.

LAMINATION A process of reinforcing fragile paper with thin, translucent, or transparent sheets. In its most common form, paper is adhered to chemically unstable plastic by sealing with heat or acidic adhesives. An inherently irreversible and destructive process.

LIGNIN A component of cell walls that provides strength and rigidity in plants. It is believed to contribute to the chemical degradation of paper. It can be removed to a large extent during manufacture, but no standards exist for what is "lignin-free."

LINT-FREE CLOTH Cloth that does not produce fuzzy residue, for example unbleached muslin or well-washed cotton flannel.

MAGNETIC DUSTCLOTH Treated cloth that captures dust particles through electrostatic or "magnetic" attraction.

MAGNETIC TAPE Thin ribbon of plastic tape coated with material containing metallic particles. Information is stored through varying localized magnetization.

MUSEUM BOARD Laminated type of mat board made from linen or cotton rags, or from deacidified and buffered paper pulp. Often used to remount pictures with lower-quality backing.

NEUTRAL Having a pH value of 7; neither acidic nor alkaline.

NITRATE FILM First generation of film, used from 1888 to 1951 for commercial motion pictures. Nitrate film yellows and embrittles with age, the silver image is oxidized, and the gelatin binder layer may become tacky. Identified by "nitrate" printed on edge and acrid odor.

OFF-GASSING The process of slowly releasing volatile materials that often contribute to the deterioration of objects. A propensity of wood and some paints that should be considered in storage and display.

OPTICAL DISK A plastic-coated disk on which information is recorded digitally as tiny pits that are read by a laser. Compact discs are small optical disks.

ORGANIC Coming from animal or plant sources, made up of protein or cellulose and other chemicals made of carbon and hydrogen.

ORMOLU Golden or gilded brass or bronze.

OXIDATION A chemical reaction that results in surface deterioration.

pH A measure of acidity and alkalinity on a scale where 7 indicates neutrality, lower numbers indicate acidity, and higher numbers indicate alkalinity. The scale is logarithmic.

PATINA Change in surface appearance attributed to use, natural and chemical aging.

PHASE BOX Custom-fitted box for storing damaged or deteriorated books upright.

PHOTOGRAPHIC ACTIVITY TEST (PAT) A test to assess the possibility that an image will fade or become stained by materials with which it comes into contact. The test gauges how reactive photographic images are to contaminants contained in materials used to display or store photographs, such as mat board and album pages. The PAT is conducted in accordance with the International Standards Organization (ISO 14523).

POLYESTER Common name for the plastic polyethylene terephthalate. Characteristics include chemical stability, transparency, and high tensile strength. Trade names include Mylar D® and Melinex®.

POLYETHYLENE A chemically stable, highly flexible, transparent or translucent plastic.

POLYPROPYLENE A chemically stable plastic of the same family as polyethylene that resists heat and is stiffer than polyethylene.

POLYVINYL CHLORIDE (PVC) A chemically unstable plastic that can emit hydrochloric acid. May also be called vinyl.

POWDER-COATED A surface coating applied via dry powder fused through heat. Seals and eliminates off-gassing.

PRESERVATION Activities that minimize chemical and physical deterioration and damage and that prevent loss of informational content. The primary goal of preservation is to prolong the existence of cultural property.

PREVENTIVE CARE Actions taken to retard deterioration and mitigate damage through maintenance procedures and provision of optimal conditions of storage, display, use, and handling.

PROVENANCE The origin or source of an object. The object's history. Same as provenience, a term which is used primarily with archaeological collections.

RAG BOARD/RAG PAPER High-quality, durable board or paper made from cotton or other textile fiber. Low in acidity; may be buffered.

RELATIVE HUMIDITY The percentage of moisture in the air relative to the maximum amount the air can hold at that temperature.

RESTORATION Conservation treatment activity aimed at returning an object to a known or assumed state, often through the addition of nonoriginal material.

REVERSIBILITY Ability to undo a process or treatment with no change to the original object. An important goal of conservation treatment that is balanced with other treatment goals and options.

SAFETY FILM A photographic film whose base is fire resistant or slow burning. Refers to acetate or polyester-based film.

SCAVENGERS Substances that remove undesirable environmental elements, such as sulfur, through chemical or physical means.

SIZINGS/SIZED Chemicals added to paper to make it less absorbent so inks will not bleed. Acidic sizings, such as alum rosin, can cause paper to deteriorate. Some sizings are not acidic and are expected to be more chemically stable.

SOLANDER BOX A protective, rigid enclosure for archival storage used primarily for works of art on paper.

STABILIZATION Conservation treatment activity aimed to maintain integrity and minimize deterioration.

TINTYPE Photograph taken directly as a positive print on a sensitized plate of enameled tin.

TREATMENT Deliberate alteration of chemical and/or physical aspects of an object in order to prolong its existence. See stabilization and restoration.

ULTRAVIOLET RADIATION Radiation of wavelengths shorter than 400nm. Found in light from the sun, sky, and most artificial light sources. It is invisible, highly energetic and has a strongly damaging effect on objects. Should be filtered from light sources.

ULTRAVIOLET FILTER A filter that can be placed over windows, skylights, and fluorescent light tubes to remove or reduce harmful ultraviolet radiation.

UNBUFFERED Containing no chemical reserve to maintain a pH range. Opposite of buffered.

Acknowledgments

Many individuals and institutions have graciously given of their time, expertise, and resources to help us produce this book. The strength of Heritage Preservation's programs lies in the partnerships that make them possible. Numerous partnerships with individuals, families, and institutions are at the heart of this book.

We are grateful for the vision and can-do attitude of Arthur W. Schultz, who seized upon the idea of making professional conservation advice more accessible to the public. Arthur made *Caring for Your Collections* a reality, and without that book there would be no *Caring for Your Family Treasures*.

Several institutions and families provided us with illustrations. Among them, special thanks to Grace Eleazer, Jon Krill, Susan Newton, and Fran Wilkins of the Winterthur Museum for guiding us through their remarkable photographic collection. At the Minnesota Historical Society, Sherelyn Ogden, Bob Herskovitz, and Eric Mortenson helped us locate delightful historical images. Thanks also to Susan Blakeney of West Lake Conservators in Skaneateles, New York, Jan Merrill-Oldham of the Harvard University Libraries, and Jonathan Thornton of the Art Conservation Department, Buffalo State College for their assistance in illustrating specific conservation issues. We are grateful to Paul Cooney and Barbara Heller of the Detroit Institute of Arts, who went "on location" for our benefit. To the numerous other families and institutions who provided images for this book (all of whom are listed in the Photograph Credits), our heartfelt thanks.

Special thanks to Maureen and Edwin Schloss for their generous support. We are also grateful to our lay reader, Grayce A. Hess, who made many helpful suggestions on the first draft.

It is our pleasure to work with the Board of Directors of Heritage Preservation, a bright and energetic group of conservation professionals who heartily pledged support to this project when it was just the seed of an idea. Thanks also to the staff and members of Heritage Preservation, particularly the support and expertise of Sonia Dingilian, Kristine Dixon, Moira Egan, Diane Mossholder and Kyra Skvir.

Lastly, thanks to the staff at Harry N. Abrams, Inc., including Harriet Whelchel, Carol Robson, Deborah Aaronson and Paul Gottlieb.

About the Advisers

They helped everyone his neighbor and everyone said to his brother,
Be of good courage.

Isaiah 41:6

We are deeply indebted to our panel of conservators who thoughtfully reviewed this manuscript for accuracy and completeness of conservation information. We thank them for their commitment to bringing the best information to you.

INGE-LISE ECKMANN is a conservator of paintings and works on paper specializing in modern and contemporary art. She is chairman of Heritage Preservation and a Fellow of both the American Institute for Conservation of Historic and Artistic Works and the International Institute for Conservation. Ms. Eckmann is a graduate of Bennington College and holds advanced degrees from the Cooperstown Graduate Program in Conservation, now the Art Conservation Department, Buffalo State College, New York. She served as chief conservator and Deputy Director for the San Francisco Museum of Modern Art from 1973 to 1996 and currently has a private practice based in Dallas, Texas.

JANE K. HUTCHINS is a textile conservator who is a Fellow of both the American Institute for Conservation of Historic and Artistic Works and the International Institute for Conservation. During the course of her career in conservation, she has been on staff at the Museum of Fine Arts, Boston, the Museum of American Textile History in North Andover, Mass., and the Cloisters of The Metropolitan Museum of Art in New York. She is currently a visiting conservator with the Detroit Institute of Arts and Principal of Tideview Conservation in Sooke, British Columbia, where she also raises sheep and llamas. She holds a B.A. from Wesleyan University and a M.S. in textile materials from North Carolina State University. Ms. Hutchins has lectured and published widely in the field as well has held numerous positions with professional organizations for more than twenty years. Among her cherished family treasures are textile books and samples from her grandmother.

DEBRA HESS NORRIS is Director and Associate Professor of Photograph Conservation for the Winterthur/University of Delaware Program in Art Conservation. She also serves as Director of the University of Delaware undergraduate program in art conservation. She has written extensively about the conservation treatment and preservation of historic and contemporary photographic materials and issues relating to emergency response and recovery. Ms. Norris received a M.S. degree in Photograph Conservation from the University of Delaware in 1977 and an interdisciplinary undergraduate degree in art history, art, and chemistry from the same institution. She has consulted on the care and preservation of photographic collections throughout the world and lectured widely on this and other related topics. She is on the boards of Heritage Preservation and the Conservation Center for Art and Historic Artifacts, a member of the National Task Force on Emergency Response, and past president of the American Institute for Conservation of Historic and Artistic Works. She is strongly committed to the importance of public education about conservation and enjoys assisting with the care of family photographs.

ROY PERKINSON is Head of Paper Conservation at the Museum of Fine Arts in Boston. He originally trained as a physicist at M.I.T. and worked for a while at Draper Laboratories while at the same time pursuing his studies in studio art at the School of the Museum of Fine Arts. Eventually he obtained a M.A. in Art History while supporting himself as a teacher at the Museum of Science. Art conservation then presented itself as the ideal synthesis of the two cultures of art and science. Since 1967, he has devoted himself to this field, although he continues to work at what he calls his "second job" as a landscape painter (he regularly shows and sells his work in oil, watercolor, and pastel). Roy's aunt generously entrusted to him dozens of family letters from the early to late nineteenth century, as well as a number of irreplaceable family photographs, and thus he has had personal experience with the demands of choosing the proper storage materials to protect and organize these precious family heirlooms.

JULIE A. REILLY is currently Associate Director and Chief Conservator for the Nebraska State Historical Society, where she directs the Gerald R. Ford Conservation Center in Omaha. She is also an Adjunct Professor for the Museum Studies Department at the University of Nebraska at Lincoln. Previously, she has worked in object conservation for the National Museum of American History, the Applied Archaeology Center of the National Park Service, the Colonial Williamsburg Foundation, and the Henry Francis du Pont Winterthur Museum and Gardens. Ms. Reilly holds a B.A. from Towson State University and a M.A. in Anthropology from the George Washington University. She has been a consulting conservator to many cultural institutions and has spoken widely on topics relating to the care and conservation of collections. Additionally, she has given a number of professional presentations and published in professional journals. A Fellow of the American Institute for Conservation of Historic and Artistic Works, Ms. Reilly is currently associate editor of their journal and a board member of Heritage Preservation. After more than fourteen years living all over the world and moving every two years, the Reilly family retains very few special treasures. This makes each one a cherished emblem of the family's history.

We are also grateful to Deborah L. Long, Head of the Objects Conservation Laboratory at the Gerald R. Ford Conservation Center, James Moss of Clockmakers Inc., Andrew Robb, Senior Photograph Conservator at The Library of Congress, Sarah D. Stauderman, Preservation Manager at the Smithsonian Institution Archives, and John R. Watson, Conservator of Instruments at The Colonial Williamsburg Foundation, for their thoughtful review of chapters pertinent to their specialties.

About Heritage Preservation

Heritage Preservation is a national nonprofit organization working to preserve America's collective heritage for present and future generations. Its programs and publications provide information from top professionals on caring for photographs, historic documents, books, works of art, buildings, natural science specimens, and family heirlooms. Members include leading museums, libraries, archives, and historic preservation organizations; through Heritage Preservation they participate in programs that benefit smaller institutions and the general public. Heritage Preservation's programs include Save Outdoor Sculpture!, the National Task Force on Emergency Response, and the Conservation Assessment Program. For more information, please visit www.heritagepreservation.org or call 1-888-388-6789.

Caring for Your Family Treasures is the third book Heritage Preservation has published to help individuals care for cherished belongings. *Caring for Your Collections*, published in 1992, contains nineteen detailed chapters written by professional conservators about various types of objects as well as issues such as security, insurance, and donations. *Caring for Your Historic House*, published in 1998, contains twenty chapters by architectural conservators and preservation practitioners about the care of old homes. Chapters cover components of the house such as roofs, interior woodwork, electrical systems, and appraisals.

Many antique clocks have beautiful artistic details.

Index

Page numbers in *italics* refer to illustrations.

Photograph and Illustration Credits

Numbers refer to page numbers.

Art Conservation Department, Buffalo State College: 36, 39, 82, 93 (middle and below), 115, 129 (above) and jacket back

Brooklyn Museum of Art: 17

Charles Gupton/Stock, Boston, Inc.: 53

City of Omaha, Nebraska: 102 (bottom), 120

Collection of Bruce P. Marshall. Photo by West Lake Conservators Ltd.: 66

Collection of Raymond and Susan Egan. Photo by West Lake Conservators Ltd.: 84

Colonial Williamsburg Foundation: 81 (above)

Courtesy Barbara Heller. Photo by Paul Cooney: 129 (below left and right) and jacket back

Courtesy Bouton and Kurtz Families. Photo by Okello Dunkley: 104

Courtesy Bouton family. Photo by Okello Dunkley: 118 (below)

Courtesy Buskey Family. Photo by Okello Dunkley: 85, 101, 103, 129 and jacket back

Courtesy Debra Hess Norris: 46, 48 (above), 76 (above)

Courtesy Dr. and Mrs. Joseph E. Corr. Photo by Textile Conservation Workshop: 74 (above)

Courtesy Harvard University Libraries: 28 (below)

Courtesy Historical Society of Long Beach, California: 35, 42 (top right), 45

Courtesy James Overbeck: 44 and jacket back

Courtesy John Birkinbine II Family Trust. Photo by Textile Conservation Workshop: 73

Courtesy John Krill: 141

Courtesy Katlan Family. Photo by A. Katlan: 21 and jacket back

Courtesy Long Family. Photo by Jane S. Long: 38

Courtesy Mary Anderson Bain. Photo by Okello Dunkley: 42 (below)

Courtesy Moira Egan and Jim Vore. Photo by Okello Dunkley: 89, 97

Courtesy National Museum of American History, Division of History of Technology Rail Collection: 122 (below right and left)

Courtesy Nichols-Buchanan Family. Photo by Okello Dunkley: 31, 42 (middle), 95

Courtesy Nichols-Buchanan Family. Photo by Susan Nichols: 80 (below), 86

Courtesy the Plains Art Museum, Fargo, N. D.: 76